**New Directions for
Community Colleges**

Arthur M. Cohen
EDITOR-IN-CHIEF

Caroline Q. Durdella
Nathan R. Durdella
ASSOCIATE EDITORS

Amy Fara Edwards
MANAGING EDITOR

Comprehensive Reform for Student Success

Nan L. Maxwell
Ann E. Person

EDITORS

Number 176 • Winter 2016
Jossey-Bass
San Francisco

Comprehensive Reform for Student Success
Nan L. Maxwell, Ann E. Person (eds.)
New Directions for Community Colleges, no. 176

Editor-in-Chief: *Arthur M. Cohen*
Associate Editors: *Caroline Q. Durdella, Nathan R. Durdella*
Managing Editor: *Amy Fara Edwards*

New Directions for Community Colleges, (ISSN 0194-3081; Online ISSN: 1536-0733), is published quarterly by Wiley Subscription Services, Inc., a Wiley Company, 111 River St., Hoboken, NJ 07030-5774 USA.

Postmaster: Send all address changes to *New Directions for Community Colleges,* John Wiley & Sons Inc., C/O The Sheridan Press, PO Box 465, Hanover, PA 17331 USA.

Information for subscribers
New Directions for Community Colleges is published in 4 issues per year. Institutional subscription prices for 2017 are:
Print & Online: US$454 (US), US$507 (Canada & Mexico), US$554 (Rest of World), €363 (Europe), £285 (UK). Prices are exclusive of tax. Asia-Pacific GST, Canadian GST/HST and European VAT will be applied at the appropriate rates. For more information on current tax rates, please go to www.wileyonlinelibrary.com/tax-vat. The price includes online access to the current and all online backfiles to January 1st 2013, where available. For other pricing options, including access information and terms and conditions, please visit www.wileyonlinelibrary.com/access.

Delivery Terms and Legal Title
Where the subscription price includes print issues and delivery is to the recipient's address, delivery terms are **Delivered at Place (DAP)**; the recipient is responsible for paying any import duty or taxes. Title to all issues transfers FOB our shipping point, freight prepaid. We will endeavour to fulfil claims for missing or damaged copies within six months of publication, within our reasonable discretion and subject to availability.

Back issues: Single issues from current and recent volumes are available at the current single issue price from cs-journals@wiley.com.

Disclaimer
The Publisher and Editors cannot be held responsible for errors or any consequences arising from the use of information contained in this journal; the views and opinions expressed do not necessarily reflect those of the Publisher and Editors, neither does the publication of advertisements constitute any endorsement by the Publisher and Editors of the products advertised.

Publisher: New Directions for Community Colleges is published by Wiley Periodicals, Inc., 350 Main St., Malden, MA 02148–5020.

Journal Customer Services: For ordering information, claims and any enquiry concerning your journal subscription please go to www.wileycustomerhelp.com/ask or contact your nearest office.
Americas: Email: cs-journals@wiley.com; Tel: +1 781 388 8598 or +1 800 835 6770 (toll free in the USA & Canada).
Europe, Middle East and Africa: Email: cs-journals@wiley.com; Tel: +44 (0) 1865 778315.
Asia Pacific: Email: cs-journals@wiley.com; Tel: +65 6511 8000.
Japan: For Japanese speaking support, Email: cs-japan@wiley.com.
Visit our Online Customer Help available in 7 languages at www.wileycustomerhelp.com/ask

Production Editor: Shreya Srivastava (email: shsrivsata@wiley.com).

Wiley's Corporate Citizenship initiative seeks to address the environmental, social, economic, and ethical challenges faced in our business and which are important to our diverse stakeholder groups. Since launching the initiative, we have focused on sharing our content with those in need, enhancing community philanthropy, reducing our carbon impact, creating global guidelines and best practices for paper use, establishing a vendor code of ethics, and engaging our colleagues and other stakeholders in our efforts. Follow our progress at www.wiley.com/go/citizenship

View this journal online at wileyonlinelibrary.com/journal/cc

Wiley is a founding member of the UN-backed HINARI, AGORA, and OARE initiatives. They are now collectively known as Research4Life, making online scientific content available free or at nominal cost to researchers in developing countries. Please visit Wiley's Content Access – Corporate Citizenship site: http://www.wiley.com/WileyCDA/Section/id-390082.html

Printed in the USA by The Sheridan Group.

Address for Editorial Correspondence: Associate Editor, *Caroline Q. Durdella, New Directions for Community Colleges,* Email: kguthrie@fsu.edu.

Abstracting and Indexing Services
The Journal is indexed by Academic Search Alumni Edition (EBSCO Publishing); Education Index/Abstracts (EBSCO Publishing); ERA: Educational Research Abstracts Online (T&F); ERIC: Educational Resources Information Center (CSC); MLA International Bibliography (MLA).

Cover design: Wiley
Cover Images: © Lava 4 images | Shutterstock

For submission instructions, subscription and all other information visit:
wileyonlinelibrary.com/journal/cc

CONTENTS

Comprehensive Reform for Student Success

In the past decade, community colleges have faced pressures from government, the private sector, and prominent foundations to "do more with less," even as new postsecondary education providers have increased competition for students and other resources. Such pressures have prompted many community college leaders to consider fundamental changes to the ways they have typically done business. With the experience of piecemeal solutions that have not often been effective or efficient, colleges are moving far beyond discreet "programs" or "interventions," and college leaders are attempting to implement comprehensive reform efforts.

Although a single, authoritative definition of "comprehensive" reform does not exist, we posit that current manifestations of it share three key components. First, student success is typically the justification for why broad changes are needed and the criterion for what constitutes successful change for today's comprehensive reform efforts. Second, such reforms are grounded in a theory of change that ties programmatic components together in an intentional and cohesive package, implemented at multiple levels throughout the college and touching the majority of students (that is, operating "at scale"). Finally, current comprehensive reform efforts call for colleges to build a culture of evidence that uses data to continuously assess programs and processes against student success, suggesting changes when benchmarks are not achieved.

Achieving the Dream (ATD) is a primary example of contemporary approaches to comprehensive reform and an important point of departure for any thorough discussion of the topic. In shaping ATD, Lumina Foundation for Education and its partners articulated an explicit theory of change behind the sweeping reform they envisioned. At the core of this theory was the development of a culture of evidence that would use data to inform program development and implementation and support continuous improvement. ATD's explicit outcome goal was measurable improvement of student success, specifically increased course and program completion (Rutschow et al., 2011).

Other public and private efforts to improve community colleges have arisen in the wake of ATD, and all share a similar focus on student success, cohesive packaging of scaled programs, and a culture of evidence. In 2010, the Bill & Melinda Gates Foundation launched the Completion by Design (CBD) initiative. CBD set an explicit goal for participating colleges to "re-

New Directions for Community Colleges, no. 176, Winter 2016 © 2016 Wiley Periodicals, Inc.
Published online in Wiley Online Library (wileyonlinelibrary.com) • DOI: 10.1002/cc.20217

structure the student experience ... build linkages and interdependencies among the systems that touch the lives of the students, and ... establish clear accountability for student success" (Pennington & Milliron, 2010, p. 3). Similarly, the Aspen Institute's College Excellence Program aims to identify and replicate campus-wide practices that significantly improve college student outcomes (Aspen Institute, 2014) and Aspen's Prize for Community College Excellence has put a spotlight on colleges that meet student success performance benchmarks.

The U.S. Department of Labor's Trade Adjustment Assistance Community College and Career Training (TAACCCT) grants program is the largest public reform effort currently underway in community colleges nationwide. Although the TAACCCT program does not explicitly state a common theory of change for all grantees, it implies such a theory in the program's embrace of measureable student success goals similar to ATD: increased credit accumulation and credential completion, as well as improved employment outcomes for students (U.S. Department of Labor, 2012). Moreover, the program encourages aspiring grantees to propose multiple programmatic components and to specify how these components will work together to support student success. Finally, the TAACCCT program requires regular performance measurement and asks grantees to describe how they will use data to support continuous program improvement.

In addition to these national programs, comprehensive reform efforts have also emerged at the state level. In some cases, change has been driven from within a state's community college system. The Virginia Community College System (VCCS) Re-Engineering Taskforce, which was established by the chancellor in 2009, seeks to "examine and rethink every aspect of [VCCS] organization and operations other than governance" (VCCS, 2010, p. 1) and provides one example of such efforts. Other state-level reforms have been driven by legislation, as in the case of Florida's statutory changes to the K–20 education code, which specified—among other things—that the state's public colleges should adopt common assessments for academic placement, implement a system of metamajors across all colleges, and counsel students into college-level courses as soon as possible. Similarly, the California legislature's establishment of the state's Early Assessment Program, although focused on assessment in high schools, has far-reaching implications for the state's community colleges.

This volume of *New Directions for Community Colleges* presents chapters that examine several contemporary comprehensive reform efforts. The reforms we discuss include state and federal government and foundation-sponsored initiatives, but all emphasize the three common elements described previously: a focus on measurable student success, an intentional and cohesive packaging of programmatic components to be implemented at scale, and a culture of evidence. Each chapter in the volume presents original analysis, discussing implications of the research for practice, and each ends with a set of recommendations for practice in community colleges.

The authors' empirical approaches provide insight on how comprehensive "interventions" can best be analyzed and the evidence presented in their chapters enhances our understanding of the promise and perils of comprehensive reform. Across the chapters, a few components emerge as critical for the success of comprehensive reform efforts, in particular, executive leadership complemented by strong faculty involvement, guided by an explicit and shared vision for success. Technology can play a key role in comprehensive reform, but the research presented here suggests that the adaptive capacity of institutions is equally critical. At least two common challenges emerge across the chapters, as well. First, the difficulty of balancing a real need for pilot-testing with the ultimate goal of scaled change. A second challenge, flowing from the first, is how to assess the impacts of a package of interventions, pieces of which touch the entire student population. Although the authors do not resolve these issues, their discussion of implications from their research helps to ensure that community college practitioners can use information from the chapters to inform their own efforts to improve student success.

The volume is organized to examine comprehensive reform from different perspectives. We set the stage with the first two chapters that take a bird's-eye view of reform: framing the problem, assessing the evidence to date, and suggesting implications for future reform efforts. Each author brings a broad perspective on the rationale for and potential of comprehensive reform, gleaned from their long tenure working with community colleges. The first chapter, by Tom Bailey, discusses current challenges facing community colleges and describes why reform must be comprehensive if the challenges are to be resolved. The second chapter, by Tom Brock, Alex Mayer, and Elizabeth Zachry Rutshow, draws lessons from two national initiatives for comprehensive reform, ATD and CBD, to suggest how rigorous evaluations can help community colleges realize the potential of comprehensive reform.

The next six chapters provide empirical assessment of a variety of reform efforts, focusing their analysis on different aspects of students' movement into and through community colleges. The first three chapters in this section discuss student preparation for and navigation through community college coursework. The first, by Nikki Edgecombe, discusses findings from an evaluation of Virginia's statewide overhaul of developmental education and the second, by Elizabeth Friedmann, Michal Kurlaender, and Alice VanOmmeren, discusses findings from an evaluation of California's statewide effort to improve college preparation while students are still in high school. In the third, Shanna Smith Jaggars and Melinda Mechur Karp discuss comprehensive new "e-advising" approaches that leverage technology to help students make choices that will improve their chances for successful program completion. The next three chapters examine the full student experience. Debra Bragg and Marianne Krismer explore the nature and structure of programs of study to facilitate retention, graduation, and workforce success. Linda Thor and Joseph Moreau illustrate how community colleges can use technology to build a student-centric teaching and learning environment at a system level. Finally, Ann Person and Nancy Thibeault describe a multistate effort to implement competency-based learning to improve student success both at the community college and in careers.

The two final chapters in the volume take a step back to consider the perspective of college practitioners in the trenches of reform. These chapters discuss the challenges that arise with leading, implementing, and learning from reform. The first, by Nan Maxwell and Ann Person, discusses the gaps that must be bridged for colleges to develop a culture of evidence that can support continuous improvement. The final chapter, by Karen Stout, provides a community college president's perspective on the practical opportunities and challenges faced in implementing comprehensive reforms.

Several individuals were instrumental in helping shape this volume, in addition to the chapter authors. Kendall Guthrie, formerly of the Bill & Melinda Gates Foundation, helped stimulate the discussion from which this volume sprang during the American Evaluation Association meetings in 2013. Nathan Durdella, our editor, pushed our thinking from volume inception through publication.

Nan L. Maxwell
Ann E. Person
Editors

References

Aspen Institute. (2014). *College Excellence Program*. Retrieved from http://www.aspen institute.org/policy-work/aspen-prize

Pennington, H., & Milliron, M. (2010). *Completion by design: Concept paper*. Seattle, WA: Bill & Melinda Gates Foundation. Retrieved from http://www.completionbydesign .org/sites/default/files/site-uploads/main-site/pdf/cbd_concept_paper.pdf

Rutschow, E. Z., Richburg-Hayes, L., Brock, T., Orr, G., Cerna, O., Cullinan, D., ... & Martin, K. (2011). *Turning the tide: Five years of Achieving the Dream in Community Colleges*. New York: MDRC. Retrieved from http://www.mdrc.org/sites/default/ files/full_593.pdf

U.S. Department of Labor, Employment and Training Administration. (2012). *Notice of availability of funds and solicitation for grant applications for Trade Adjustment Assistance Community College and Career Training Grants Program*, SGA/DFA PY-12-10. Retrieved from http://www.doleta.gov/grants/pdf/taaccct_sga_dfa_py_12_10.pdf

Virginia Community College System. (2010). *Report of Virginia's Community Colleges' Re-Engineering Task Force*. Retrieved from http://rethink.vccs.edu/wp-content/uploads/ 2010/03/ReengineeringReport-Nov2010.pdf

NAN L. MAXWELL *and* ANN E. PERSON *are senior researchers at Mathematica Policy Research.*

1

This chapter examines why typical reforms at community colleges in recent years have not improved institutional graduation rates. It argues that substantially increasing college completion requires comprehensive institutional reform with a focus on measurable student success, an intentional and cohesive package of programmatic components, and a culture of evidence.

The Need for Comprehensive Reform: From Access to Completion

Thomas Bailey

Over the last few decades, the importance of a college education has grown both for society and for individuals. This is reflected in the large earnings gap between individuals with a high school degree and those with a postsecondary credential (Belfield & Bailey, 2011). However, most students who start in community colleges never complete a degree or certificate. This constitutes a failure for those students to achieve their goals and represents a loss of potential earning power and economic growth and activity for the economy as a whole. Although students experience earnings gains by accumulating credits without graduating, they get a significant additional increase upon completing a credential (Belfield & Bailey, 2011).

This chapter considers what types of reform and innovation are most likely to increase the chances that community college students will complete their credentials. It first discusses the shift from a reform focus on college access to one emphasizing college completion; it then reviews the barriers to improvement in college completion, arguing that community colleges have been organized to expand enrollment to a greater part of the population, but that organization is not well suited to promote completion of credentials. The chapter also reviews the types of reforms that have been introduced to improve completion and shows that these interventions have had limited effects. Significant improvements in college completion will require more comprehensive reforms that address the organizational barriers to student success. The editors of this volume have emphasized three elements of such reform: a focus on measurable student success, an intentional and cohesive package of programmatic components, and a culture of

NEW DIRECTIONS FOR COMMUNITY COLLEGES, no. 176, Winter 2016 © 2016 Wiley Periodicals, Inc.
Published online in Wiley Online Library (wileyonlinelibrary.com) • DOI: 10.1002/cc.20218

evidence. In addition, to have an impact on college completion rates, reforms must be scaled to include most of the target student population, and they must address the entire student experience in college.

The Growing Focus on College Completion

Public higher education policy in the latter half of the 20th century was designed to open college to the large majority of the U.S. population. The Servicemen's Readjustment Act of 1944 (also known as the GI Bill); the California Master Plan for Higher Education of 1960; the Higher Education Act of 1965, which established the Pell Grant; and the rapid growth of community colleges were all designed to make college accessible for all students. They focused on reducing the cost of college to the student and, in the case of community colleges, established open access, and flexible, convenient colleges in reasonable proximity to a large majority of the population, including especially groups traditionally underrepresented in postsecondary education. At the same time, technology and the characteristics of work were also changing, resulting in increasing demand for a more educated workforce. These factors contributed to increases in college enrollment, such that by the turn of the century, over 75% of high school graduates had attended some postsecondary institution by their mid-20s (author's calculations using data from the Education Longitudinal Study of 2002, National Center for Education Statistics 2002).

But over the last 20 years, educators and policy makers have turned their attention to college completion. Although progress on enrollment cast community college performance in a positive light, the more recent focus on completion yields a much more negative image. In 2000, the U.S. Department of Education began publishing 3-year graduation rates for most colleges that tracked cohorts of first-time, full-time college students who started in community college. Graduation rates for many colleges were in the single digits and teens. The overall 3-year completion rate for community college students nationwide was 24% for the 2000 cohort and 20% for the 2010 cohort (National Center for Education Statistics, 2014, Table 326.20). Researchers, college representatives, and policy makers have criticized this rate as incomplete and misleading (Bailey, Jenkins, & Leinbach, 2005). But more comprehensive measures from the 1990s showed that less than 40% of entering community college students completed any degree or certificate from any college within 6 years (author's calculation from the National Education Longitudinal Study of 1988, National Center for Education Statistics [1988]).

In response to low completion rates, educators, reformers, policy makers, and foundations called for a concerted effort to increase the number of individuals with college degrees and certificates, which has come to be called the "completion agenda." The Obama administration, Lumina Foundation, and the Bill & Melinda Gates Foundation all called for ambitious

NEW DIRECTIONS FOR COMMUNITY COLLEGES • DOI: 10.1002/cc

increases in the number of college graduates by the middle of the 2020s (Bailey, 2012; Lumina Foundation, 2010). Many states have set goals designed to contribute proportionately to the national goals (Complete College America, 2015). In addition, the federal government and multiple foundations have funded extensive research and reform portfolios.

Barriers to College Completion

Students and colleges will need to overcome a number of challenges to achieve the ambitious goals of the completion agenda. Community college students tend to face many serious barriers to success: low-income students are significantly overrepresented in community colleges (Carnevale & Strohl, 2010) and most need to strengthen both academic and nonacademic skills.

Despite the substantial needs of their student populations, community colleges are given comparatively few resources. In 2011, public 2-year institutions spent about $8,100 (in 2011 dollars) per student; in contrast, institutions in the public master's sector spent just over $12,000 (College Board, 2014, Figure 19A). Thus, the colleges whose students have the greatest needs have the fewest resources to address those needs.

In addition, community colleges are not well organized to promote completion. The features that have allowed community colleges to expand access may not be optimal to promote completion of programs that support deep student learning and that prepare students for success. Bailey, Jaggars, and Jenkins, 2015 refer to the traditional community college model as the "cafeteria" or "self-service" college. In this model, colleges provide many options and services, but students must find their own way through often complex or ill-defined programs. Such cafeteria organization creates problems in three areas: the structure of college-level programs, the intake process and student supports, and developmental education.

Structure of Programs.   Community colleges are designed to facilitate enrollment for a heterogeneous student population with a wide variety of goals. Most offer an extensive array of courses and programs, and students have broad flexibility to decide when to enroll and at what intensity, what programs to pursue, and which courses to take within those programs. Students can easily stop out and presumably return to college when it is convenient. The potential for transfer to many different 4-year colleges further complicates students' choices. Research in behavioral economics demonstrates that individuals do not do a good job of making decisions when faced with such large sets of complex and ill-defined choices (Bailey et al., 2015; Scott-Clayton, 2011).

Intake and Supports.   With limited resources, community colleges are unable to provide comprehensive advising to all students to help them navigate these complex institutions. There are often many hundreds of students for every counselor or advisor. As a result, college intake and advising often consist of a brief face-to-face or online orientation and a short meeting (not always mandatory) with an advisor, focused on registering for the first semester's courses. Most colleges do not provide an organized process to help students form long-term goals and design an academic program to achieve those goals. Rather, students must recognize when they need help and seek it out on their own (Bailey et al., 2015; Grubb, 2006; Jaggars & Fletcher, 2014; Jaggars & Karp, Chapter 5 in this volume). Moreover, most colleges do not closely monitor students' progress toward their goals or through programs.

Developmental Education.   Students' progress is often stalled by lengthy developmental course sequences. All community colleges assess students' academic skills at entry and, based on these assessments, college staff advise the majority of students to enroll in developmental education courses (Bailey, Jeong, & Cho, 2010). Yet traditional developmental education is often not able to prepare students to succeed in college-level courses (Jaggars & Stacey, 2014). Most students do not complete their assigned sequences, and enrolling in developmental education courses does not, on average, increase the probability that students will complete college-level courses or achieve other desired outcomes (Bailey, Jaggars, & Scott-Clayton, 2013).

In short, community college students face many barriers to completion, and the funding, structure, and organization of the colleges make it difficult to help students overcome those barriers. These issues will have to be addressed if colleges are to increase their completion rates and overall performance substantially.

The Limitations of Traditional Reform

During the last 2 decades, community colleges have attempted many reforms to improve student success (Bailey & Morest, 2006). The Achieving the Dream: Community Colleges Count (ATD) initiative illustrates the fundamental characteristics of the types of reforms that have predominated in this period. (Brock, Mayer, & Rutschow, Chapter 2 of this volume, discuss ATD in detail.) In 2004, Lumina Foundation for Education and its partners initiated ATD and funded 27 colleges to carry out a series of reforms with the explicit goal of improving student outcomes. Subsequently, several hundred colleges participated in ATD. The developers articulated an underlying theory of action urging colleges to use their longitudinal data to identify barriers to student success and apply evidence-based reforms to correct those barriers, leading to increased completions. In addition to financial support, ATD colleges benefited from technical assistance by coaches and researchers and participated in workshops and conferences sponsored by ATD. Emblematic of the completion agenda, ATD represented an ambitious and well-funded initiative designed to introduce reforms that would lead to increases in college completion (Achieving the Dream, n.d.).

In 2011, MDRC, in partnership with the Community College Research Center, published a report, describing the interventions and the first 5 years of ATD experience among 26 of the 27 initial college participants (Rutschow et al., 2011). The colleges introduced reforms in three broad areas: student support services, instructional support (such as tutoring), and changes in classroom instruction. Every college had some intervention devoted to improving outcomes for developmental students and the majority of ATD reforms focused on helping students during the early stages of their college experience.

In general, the early ATD experience illustrates the dominant characteristics of community college reform during the completion agenda era. Colleges have been willing, and are often enthusiastic, to experiment with new practices and strategies but have frequently directed them at one segment of the student experience (usually the beginning); and they have generally reached a relatively small number of students (although "light-touch" efforts have sometimes reached larger groups of students). The ATD evaluation (Rutschow et al., 2011) found that despite enthusiastic reform activity, completion rates on average had not increased for participating colleges at the end of 5 years. Outcomes from a 2009 follow-up program, the Developmental Education Initiative funded by the Bill & Melinda Gates Foundation and designed to scale up promising practices introduced by ATD, were similarly disappointing (Quint, Jaggars, Byndloss, & Magazinnik, 2013).

Evaluations of targeted reforms of the type implemented by the ATD colleges show that even when they have positive effects on short-term outcomes—such as enrollment and success in entry-level college courses—the benefits to student participants tend to fade over subsequent semesters. This was the case in a rigorous evaluation of learning communities in six community colleges conducted by the National Center for Postsecondary Research (Visher, Weiss, Weissman, Rudd, & Wathington, 2012).

The Accelerated Learning Program (ALP) developed at the Community College of Baltimore County provides another example of an intervention with short-term positive outcomes but no effect on graduation rates. ALP is a remediation model in which students referred to developmental reading are placed into a college-level English course with an additional academic support section. An evaluation showed that ALP students were 32% more likely to complete the first college-level English course within 1 year than similar students in standard developmental reading (Cho, Kopko, Jenkins, & Jaggars, 2012). But despite the encouraging success of ALP, the 3-year graduation rate for first-time, full-time students for the college in the years following its introduction did not improve (National Center for Education Statistics, n.d.). Although the student body at the college changed over this period, and the 3-year completion rate is not an ideal measure, these data suggest that the college has not been able to convert success in remedial reforms into broad institutional improvement.

NEW DIRECTIONS FOR COMMUNITY COLLEGES • DOI: 10.1002/cc

These examples suggest that isolated interventions, even when they yield positive outcomes for participants, do not generally improve institutional graduation rates. National trends in graduation rates support this conclusion. As noted previously, data from the 1990s showed that less than 40% of entering community college students graduated from any institutions within 6 years. Data from the National Student Clearinghouse for the cohort of students who entered in 2007 showed that 38% had completed a degree or certificate within 6 years (Shapiro et al., 2015).

Two broad reasons help explain why institutional aggregates and broad measures of college performance have been immune to focused reforms and the college completion agenda. First, pilot projects rarely scale. Initiatives usually start by testing a practice using a small number of students, with the expectation that a successful practice will be used on all students in the target population. Pilot implementation makes sense in theory but rarely works in practice. Sometimes initial grant funding runs out, and the initiative fades away. Small pilots can rely on a small group of activist faculty, administrators, and stakeholders who are enthusiastic about reform, and they can be carried out without disrupting normal practices at an institution. But scaling requires engagement of a much larger segment of the faculty and may require budgeting, schedule, personnel, and administrative changes.

The ATD evaluation (Rutschow et al., 2011) showed that 52% of the interventions reached less than 10% of their target populations, and only about one third reached a quarter of them. The larger scale interventions tended to be what the authors referred to as "light touch," providing services for 5 or fewer hours. Such limited penetration cannot be expected to increase the overall institutional performance numbers. And, as noted, the explicit and funded effort to scale apparently successful interventions through the Developmental Education Initiative was similarly disappointing (Quint et al., 2013).

The second reason why discrete interventions might not move institutional performance measures is that in most cases, they address only one segment of a student's experience in college, rather than touching each progressive phase of the student experience. This is known as the problem of vertical scaling. For example, as was the case with ATD, many reforms focus on developmental education, the first stage of many students' college careers. But if a student's college-level program is difficult to follow, and if the student does not continue to get support and guidance, any early benefit from the reform is likely to dissipate as the student progresses. Belfield, Crosta, and Jenkins 2013 conducted a simulation to test the effect of specific reforms on overall graduation rates. They found that a 20% increase in the share of students who complete a first college-level math course would generate only a 2.5% increase in the graduation rate.

This simulation and the research cited earlier suggest that substantially improving rates of student progression and completion requires changes in practice throughout students' college experience, not just at the front end or any one segment. Indeed, although students deemed college-ready upon entry are more successful than those referred to developmental courses, the majority of each group do not end up earning a college credential, suggesting that even students judged to be academically prepared face barriers to success in college-level coursework. To state the problem differently, many of the initial reforms motivated by the completion agenda were in effect not designed to promote completion but rather to improve an intermediate step. Improving the intermediate outcomes only had modest effects on overall completion. Thus although these colleges may have had measurable student success goals (as the comprehensive model suggests), they were the wrong goals.

The Need for Comprehensive Reform

To make significant institution-wide increases in completion, colleges must first focus on the appropriate measures of student success. It is important not just to measure the outcomes for the small number of students in a pilot program or intermediate outcomes that do not necessarily lead to institutional change. Second, colleges must have a culture of evidence that leads them to act on the measurable student outcomes. Substantial improvement requires a continuous process of reform and assessment of evidence of improvement that must become embedded in the college culture. Finally, reform cannot be limited to a small group of students or one segment of the student experience. In summary, comprehensive reform requires the three elements that form the conceptual foundation of this volume: a focus on measurable student success, a culture of evidence, and an intentional and cohesive package of programmatic components.

The guided pathways model is one example of a comprehensive reform that combines these three elements (Bailey et al., 2015; Bragg & Kismer, Chapter 6 of this volume). It is composed of an intentional and cohesive package of components, built around the development of simplified, well-organized, and easy-to-understand college-level programs of study. In this model, the college intake process is organized first to help students choose a program of study and then to address academic weaknesses that would prevent students from succeeding in their chosen program. The model is explicitly designed to support students throughout their college career by helping them choose a program, enter the program, complete the program, and make a successful transition to subsequent education or employment, and it emphasizes the need to monitor students' progress, giving frequent feedback and support as needed.

There are a growing number of examples of comprehensive reforms that incorporate many elements of the guided pathways model. Perhaps the most complete example is Guttman Community College, which is part of the City University of New York (CUNY). Guttman was created to use research-based reforms to improve measurable student outcomes. The college developed a comprehensive design that combines enhanced advising, expanded services to help students choose majors, significant instructional reform, and profound curricular redesign and simplification. Students take a common first-year curriculum and choose from a small selection of programs during their second year. The college's designers selected the fields for these programs of study based on an analysis of the needs of the local labor market. One purpose of the common first-year curriculum is to guide students through the process of choosing an appropriate program of study. This includes exposure to workplaces in related fields, and visits to bachelor's degree programs at 4-year CUNY colleges (Weinbaum, Rodriguez, & Bauer-Maglin, 2013). Each associate degree program is also designed to allow students to transfer to any of CUNY's many nearby 4-year colleges. Guttman is relatively new, so it has not been rigorously evaluated, but the 3-year graduation rate was 48% for the college's first cohort, which is more than twice the graduation rate for CUNY community college students overall. Although Guttman students are similar demographically to CUNY students, there may be unmeasured student characteristics that account for some of this difference. Nevertheless, initial results are encouraging and the college faculty and administrators are committed to continuing to improve their services based on evolving evidence on student outcomes.

City Colleges of Chicago (CCC) provides another example of a scaled comprehensive reform using guided pathways. In 2013, CCC leadership developed a 5-year strategic plan designed to double graduation rates and further increase awards and 4-year transfers. The reform created clearly structured programmatic pathways that are aligned with requirements for success in careers and further education and that have integrated supports to help students enter and complete a program of study as quickly as possible. Starting in fall 2014, all degree-seeking students were required to choose 1 of 10 focus areas (each aligned with a major area of occupational demand in Chicago) and to follow a default full-program plan created by faculty and advisors for each program. CCC advisors monitor students' progress along their program pathways, providing regular feedback to all students and support for those not adequately progressing. Since 2013, the CCC 3-year graduation rate has increased from 7% to 15%.

The Accelerated Study in Associate Programs (ASAP) is another CUNY reform that follows the student from registration to graduation. This program combines extensive advising, some financial assistance, curricular reform, and a requirement to attend full time. The program puts a strong emphasis on frequent counseling, both to help students choose their programs and to keep them on track toward completion. A random assignment evaluation by MDRC found that over a 3-year period, 40% of all ASAP students had earned a degree from any college, compared to only 22% of the control group (Scrivener et al., 2015). Although ASAP includes all three elements of the comprehensive model articulated in this volume, by 2015, ASAP had not enrolled enough students for outcomes to be reflected in overall college graduation rates, but the positive evaluation results prompted the New York State and City governments to allocate $77 million in new money for 4 years to expand ASAP to 25,000 students by 2019. One college, Bronx Community College, will enroll all of their students in ASAP.

Conclusion

The current volume articulates a model of comprehensive change that includes a focus on measurable student success, an intentional and cohesive package of programmatic components, and a culture of evidence. All of these elements are clearly present in the three examples described in the previous section. In all of these cases, the colleges and districts are focused primarily on student completion, the underlying theories of change are based on combining programmatic practices that support and guide students throughout their college careers, and the institutions are committed to tracking student progress and using evidence on student progress and program effectiveness to improve graduation rates.

A theme running through all of the chapters in this volume is the limited effect on student completion of narrowly targeted reforms that either treat too few people or are limited to one segment of the student experience. In contrast, the comprehensive models discussed here and in the rest of this volume, as exemplified by the guided pathways model, are fundamentally based on the integration of a set of coordinated reforms.

But whether a college chooses to develop guided pathways or other comprehensive models of reform, the college will face a variety of barriers to successful implementation. If reforms are to comprise a cohesive package of coordinated reforms that work with students throughout their college careers, faculty must be willing to work collectively within and across programs and departments. This may come into conflict with a culture of faculty autonomy. Similarly, advisors must also work closely with faculty; a collaboration that is weak in many colleges. Ultimately, comprehensive reform will require 2- and 4-year colleges to better coordinate their programs so that coherent pathways can be developed that span the transfer process. Such collaborations and broad institutional policy changes typically have been missing from higher education. The chapters in the volume present many suggestions about how to overcome those barriers.

References

Achieving the Dream. (n.d.) About us. Retrieved from http://achievingthedream.org/about-us

Bailey, T. (2012). Can community colleges achieve ambitious graduation goals? In A. Kelly & M. Schneider (Eds.), *Getting to graduation: The completion agenda in higher education* (pp. 73–101). Baltimore, MD: The Johns Hopkins University Press.

Bailey, T. R., Jaggars, S. S., & Jenkins, D. (2015). *Redesigning America's community colleges: A clearer path to student success.* Cambridge, MA: Harvard University Press.

Bailey, T., Jaggars, S. S., & Scott-Clayton, J. (2013). *Characterizing the effectiveness of developmental education: A response to recent criticism.* New York, NY: Columbia University, Teachers College, Community College Research Center.

Bailey, T., Jenkins, D., & Leinbach, T. (2005). *Is student success labeled institutional failure? Student goals and graduation rates in the accountability debate at community colleges (CCRC Working Paper No. 1).* New York, NY: Columbia University, Teachers College, Community College Research Center.

Bailey, T., Jeong, D. W., & Cho, S. W. (2010). Referral, enrollment, and completion in developmental education sequences in community colleges. *Economics of Education Review, 29*(2), 255–270. doi: 10.1016/j.econedurev.2009.09.002

Bailey, T., & Morest, V. S. (2006). Introduction: Defending the community college equity agenda. In T. Bailey & V. S. Morest (Eds.), *Defending the community college equity agenda* (pp. 1–27). Baltimore, MD: The Johns Hopkins University Press.

Belfield, C., & Bailey, T. (2011). The benefits of attending community college: A review of the evidence. *Community College Review, 39*(1), 46–68. doi: 10.1177/0091552110395575

Belfield, C., Crosta, P., & Jenkins, D. (2013). *Can community colleges afford to improve completion? Measuring the costs and efficiency effects of college reforms (CCRC Working Paper No. 55).* New York, NY: Columbia University, Teachers College, Community College Research Center.

Carnevale, A. P., & Strohl, J. (2010). How increasing college access is increasing inequality, and what to do about it. In R. D. Kahlenberg (Ed.), *Rewarding strivers: Helping low-income students succeed in college* (pp. 71–190). New York, NY: Century Foundation Press.

Cho, S. W., Kopko, E., Jenkins, D., & Jaggars, S. S. (2012). *New evidence of success of community college remedial English students: Tracking the outcomes of students in the Accelerated Learning Program (ALP) (CCRC Working Paper No. 53).* New York, NY: Columbia University, Teachers College, Community College Research Center.

College Board. (2014). *Trends in college pricing.* Retrieved from http://trends.collegeboard.org/

Complete College America. (2015). *The Alliance of States.* Retrieved from http://completecollege.org/the-alliance-of-states/

Grubb, N. (2006). The limits of "training for now:" Lessons from information technology certification. In T. Bailey & V. S. Morest (Eds.), *Defending the community college equity agenda* (pp. 195–222). Baltimore, MD: The Johns Hopkins University Press.

Jaggars, S. S., & Fletcher, J. (2014). *Redesigning the student intake and information provision processes at a large comprehensive community college (CCRC Working Paper No. 72).* New York, NY: Community College Research Center, Teachers College, Columbia University.

Jaggars, S. S., & Stacey, G. W. (2014). *What we know about developmental education outcomes (CCRC Practitioner Packet).* New York, NY: Columbia University, Teachers College, Community College Research Center.

Lumina Foundation for Education. (2010). *A stronger nation through higher education: How and why Americans must achieve a "big goal" for college attainment.* Retrieved from https://www.cpp.edu/~research/rsp/documents/A_stronger_nation_000.pdf

National Center for Education Statistics. (1988). *Education Longitudinal Study of 1988.* Retrieved from http://nces.ed.gov/surveys/nels88/

National Center for Education Statistics. (2002). *Education Longitudinal Study of 2002.* Retrieved from http://nces.ed.gov/surveys/els2002/

National Center for Education Statistics. (n.d.). *Integrated Postsecondary Education Data System's Graduation Rate Survey (GRS)*. Retrieved from https://nces.ed.gov/ipeds/

National Center for Education Statistics. (2014). *Table 326.20. Graduation rate from first institution attended within 150 percent of normal time for first-time, full-time degree/certificate-seeking students at 2-year postsecondary institutions, by race/ethnicity, sex, and control of institution: Selected cohort entry years, 2000 through 2010*. Retrieved from http://nces.ed.gov/programs/digest/d14/tables/dt14_326.20.asp

Quint, J. C., Jaggars, S. S., Byndloss, C. D., & Magazinnik, A. (2013). *Bringing developmental education to scale: Lessons from the developmental education initiative*. New York, NY: MDRC.

Rutschow, E. Z., Richburg-Hayes, L., Brock, T., Orr, G., Cerna, O., Cullinan, D., . . . Martin, K. (2011). *Turning the tide: Five years of Achieving the Dream in community colleges*. New York, NY: MDRC.

Scott-Clayton, J. (2011). *The shapeless river: Does a lack of structure inhibit students' progress at community colleges?* (CCRC Working Paper No. 25, Assessment of Evidence Series). New York, NY: Columbia University, Teachers College, Community College Research Center.

Scrivener, S., Weiss, M. J., Ratledge, A., Rudd, T., Sommo, C., & Fresques, H. (2015). *Doubling graduation rates: Three-year effects of CUNY's accelerated study in associate programs (ASAP) for developmental education students*. New York, NY: MDRC.

Shapiro, D., Dundar, A., Wakhungu, P. K., Yuan, X., Nathan, A., & Hwang, Y. (2015). *Completing college: A national view of student attainment rates—fall 2009 cohort* (Signature Report No. 10). Herndon, VA: National Student Clearinghouse Research Center.

Visher, M. G., Weiss, M. J., Weissman, E., Rudd, T., & Wathington, H. D. (with Teres, J., & Fong, K.). (2012). *The effects of learning communities for students in developmental education: A synthesis of findings from six community colleges*. New York, NY: National Center for Postsecondary Research.

Weinbaum, A., Rodriguez, C., & Bauer-Maglin, N. (2013). *Rethinking community college for the 21st century*. Retrieved from https://www.academia.edu/4692197/Rethinking_Community_College_for_the_21st_Century_The_New_Community_College_at_CUNY

THOMAS BAILEY *is the director of the Community College Research Center and the George and Abby O'Neill Professor of Economics and Education at Teachers College, Columbia University.*

NEW DIRECTIONS FOR COMMUNITY COLLEGES • DOI: 10.1002/cc

2

This chapter explores the role that research and evaluation play in supporting comprehensive reform in community colleges, focusing on lessons from two major initiatives: Achieving the Dream and Completion by Design.

Using Research and Evaluation to Support Comprehensive Reform

Thomas Brock, Alexander K. Mayer, Elizabeth Zachry Rutschow

As described in Chapter 1, efforts to reform community colleges are driven in large part by studies showing that many entering students do not earn degrees. In response, many states and institutions are working to understand why so many students struggle and are developing and implementing strategies for improvement. This chapter focuses on two major foundation-led initiatives that emphasized the use of research and data in making comprehensive reforms: Achieving the Dream (ATD), launched in 2004 by Lumina Foundation for Education; and Completion by Design (CBD), launched in 2011 by the Bill & Melinda Gates Foundation.

Although ATD and CBD are distinct initiatives, they contain many common features. For example, both had a primary goal of helping community colleges increase the academic success of their students. Both placed a premium on gathering and reviewing data to identify areas for improvement and on developing and implementing new policies, programs, and strategies. Both awarded grants and gave technical assistance to community colleges to help them achieve their objectives. This chapter describes the two initiatives and their lessons to date, with a particular emphasis on the role that research and evaluation can play in supporting comprehensive reform.

The First Generation of Reform: Achieving the Dream

"Know thyself." These simple words—attributed to ancient Greek philosophers—suggest that deep self-knowledge offers the path to

The views expressed in this paper do not necessarily represent the views of the federal government or Brock's employer.

NEW DIRECTIONS FOR COMMUNITY COLLEGES, no. 176, Winter 2016 © 2016 Wiley Periodicals, Inc.
Published online in Wiley Online Library (wileyonlinelibrary.com) • DOI: 10.1002/cc.20219

self-improvement. ATD was founded on a similar premise. To achieve higher graduation rates and make other improvements, the initiative sponsors, including Lumina Foundation and several national organizations it chose as partners, believed that community colleges first had to look at their own data to see how many students were successfully navigating the system or encountering roadblocks, and to learn whether certain subgroups of students—whether defined by race/ethnicity, income, or other characteristics—experienced more academic difficulty than others (Rutschow et al., 2011). Today, with advances in automated record-keeping systems, this type of review does not seem revolutionary, but at the time ATD was launched, very few community colleges had the research capacity to track students' progress over time or to break down their data to identify gaps in achievement between subgroups.

ATD set out to enhance colleges' analytic capacity and, in the process, encourage them to develop and implement strategies to serve students more effectively. The initiative sponsors issued a request for proposals inviting community colleges to participate and selected 27 institutions to embark on a five-step improvement process. (One college subsequently withdrew, leaving the 26 that are the focus of this chapter.). First, college leadership had to commit to making changes in institutional policies and resource allocations that they believed would lead to improved student outcomes. Second, the college had to collect and analyze student data, including conducting a longitudinal analysis of student outcomes and disaggregating such outcomes by race/ethnicity, Pell Grant receipt (a proxy for low-income status), and other background characteristics. Third, the college was expected to engage faculty, staff, and other stakeholders in using the data to diagnose problems and generate potential solutions. Fourth, the college was supposed to implement strategies to improve student outcomes and evaluate how well its strategies were working. Fifth, the college was expected to institutionalize effective strategies and eliminate ineffective ones and to consider student success when reviewing its programs and making budgetary decisions.

ATD provided each college with a number of supports, including $450,000 over 5 years and coaches to help guide the data analysis and institutional change processes. The colleges were asked to focus on making improvements on five key measures of student success:

1. Completion of developmental courses and progression to credit-bearing courses
2. Completion of introductory college courses in English and math
3. Completion of attempted courses with a grade "C" or better
4. Persistence from semester to semester and year to year
5. Attainment of college credentials

These measures were chosen because they were considered good indicators of students' academic progress. When the initiative was launched, neither Lumina nor its partner organizations knew how long it might take community colleges to make improvements, but most believed colleges would "move the needle" on these indicators within several years if they remained committed to the ATD process.

Findings from the Early Implementation of ATD.   The first group of 26 colleges began their ATD work in 2004. Over the next 5 years, an evaluation led by MDRC and the Community College Research Center (CCRC) found that ATD largely succeeded in helping colleges adopt the five-step improvement process. Most of the 26 colleges improved their internal research capacity, created more sophisticated systems for data collection and analysis, and enhanced their overall ability to track students' progress. These represented important attitudinal and technological shifts at a time when other community colleges across the United States were more likely to use institutional research functions for routine reporting on student enrollment rather than tracking students' academic progress. ATD colleges repeatedly noted that ATD played an important role in influencing these changes. About three out of four colleges reported that the initiative had some influence on their development of a "culture of evidence" and on their educational practices. Some colleges also noted efforts that were important to making reforms, such as accreditation reviews or Title V or TRIO grants. ATD was often seen as complementary to these efforts, even when it was not seen as the main agent of reform (Rutschow et al., 2011).

To illustrate, when ATD began, only eight of the original 26 colleges had strong institutional research departments with the capacity to regularly track student outcomes. By spring 2009, 18 had hired additional research staff, improved their information technology systems, and developed data capabilities to record students' progress from semester to semester and year to year. Colleges reported that their participation in ATD increased their respect for data analysis as a tool for identifying barriers to students' progress. By spring 2009, three fourths of the ATD colleges were tracking students longitudinally, and most were disaggregating their data to uncover important differences in academic progress between student subgroups. The colleges used this information to design new interventions and strategies that they believed would lead to greater student success.

Consistent with the early reform approach discussed in Chapter 1, most ATD colleges implemented a number of discrete interventions aimed at improving students' achievement. Sometimes the interventions represented new programs or services (such as learning communities or student success courses), whereas at other times, they represented policy changes (e.g., requiring incoming students in need of developmental education to take these courses right away). A few colleges developed a suite of interconnected interventions, such as targeting the most needy developmental students with multiple supports, such as intensive advising, student success courses, and supplemental instruction. Generally speaking, however, most colleges tried many different things and did not have a unified theory of action linking their interventions.

The evaluation revealed that most of the strategies implemented by the ATD colleges were small in scale, reaching less than 10% of their intended target population. For example, a college with several thousand students may have served about 100 students in a learning communities program (an intervention that involved placing students into cohorts that took two or more courses together, sometimes with supplemental advising or support). Strategies that were scaled to 25% or more of the targeted student populations tended to be lighter touch interventions, defined as programs that engaged students for 5 or fewer hours over the course of a semester. A typical example was a 2- or 3-hour orientation program that welcomed students to the college and explained the college's services and expectations. Another finding was that most ATD colleges had difficulty engaging a broad swath of faculty. Typically, a core group worked intensively on the initiative and was committed to making changes, but adjunct and part-time faculty—who carry a heavy portion of the teaching load at most community colleges—were rarely involved.

The MDRC/CCRC evaluation tracked the five institution-wide measures of student success over a 5-year period to determine whether significant changes in student outcomes occurred. One indicator, completion rates for students in gatekeeper English courses, registered modest improvement. Other indicators—including average completion rates for students in developmental English, developmental math, and college-level math—remained relatively flat, as did average rates of persistence in college and graduation. Few changes were seen in the academic outcomes of particular subgroups defined by race, ethnicity, and income (Rutschow et al., 2011).

It is worth underscoring that these findings represent averages across all 26 ATD colleges and that a small group of colleges performed much better or worse than average. For instance, although one college saw a 15 percentage point decrease in the developmental English completion rates, another showed a nearly 12 percentage point increase. Three colleges consistently ranked among the top improvers. In a follow-up study, MDRC and CCRC explored whether any practices set these three colleges apart. Although no clear patterns emerged, the research team noted that the three colleges concentrated on developmental education students, adopted multiple intervention strategies for these students (for example, increased instructional supports such as tutoring and supplemental instruction), and expanded the interventions in later years to reach larger numbers. Targeted professional development for faculty and staff helped support these efforts (Mayer et al., 2014).

In hindsight, there may have been a mismatch between the institution-wide measures used to evaluate ATD and the small-scale, narrowly targeted interventions implemented at most ATD colleges. The evaluation was not designed to measure the effectiveness of specific interventions because this seemed incompatible with comprehensive reform. However, even if the interventions made a positive impact on the students who participated, these impacts would have been difficult to detect among the much larger number of students enrolled in the colleges. The vast majority of students either experienced business as usual or experienced changes that were too subtle to affect course completion, persistence, or other outcomes.

Although the first group of colleges to participate in ATD may not have seen the hoped-for changes in student outcomes, they played a critical role in advancing how education policy makers, practitioners, and researchers thought about comprehensive reform. At the time ATD began, little reliable evidence existed on specific interventions to improve student outcomes, let alone on how to transform an institution. It is worth noting that the U.S. Department of Education's What Works Clearinghouse—which serves as a repository for reliable evidence on the effectiveness of education interventions—began reviewing intervention studies in postsecondary education only in 2012. ATD deserves credit for raising awareness of the challenges community college students faced, supporting a "first wave" of interventions like learning communities and student success courses, and sowing seeds for more integrated and comprehensive reforms.

The Second Generation of Reform: Completion by Design

The Bill & Melinda Gates Foundation issued a request for proposals for colleges to participate in CBD in 2011. Following a national site selection process, the foundation awarded grants to several groups of community colleges (known as cadres) to work together on planning and implementing reforms within particular states: the eight campuses of Miami Dade College in Florida, five colleges in North Carolina, and three colleges in Ohio. (A Texas cadre was also formed, but did not continue into the implementation phase.) Notably, all of the CBD states and many of the institutions had been active in ATD and drew upon their experience to launch their CBD activities. The Gates Foundation pledged $35 million to the initiative over 5 years, divided into a 12-month planning phase, a 2- to 3-year implementation phase, and a final scaling phase.

CBD sought to learn from and build on the ATD experience in several ways. First, it used the ATD database to identify factors that contribute to or impede student success in community colleges. This led to the development of a "loss and momentum" framework, which identified risks and opportunities for students at four critical phases of their college experience: connection (including application and intake to the college), entry (choosing a program of study and passing introductory courses), progress (persisting in college and accumulating credits toward a degree), and completion (earning a credential or transferring to a four-year institution). The loss and momentum framework challenged colleges to consider the full range of student needs and to address an entire spectrum of organizational and administrative factors—from resources to institutional leadership to state policy—that could influence student outcomes (Bill & Melinda Gates Foundation, 2010).

Second, CBD challenged colleges to move beyond the small-scale interventions that characterized ATD and focused on bringing greater structure and coherence to the community college experience by creating program pathways. Specifically, CBD leaders encouraged colleges to map out what students needed to do to earn a degree in the shortest amount of time in popular fields, such as psychology, business, and health careers. Colleges were also encouraged to integrate student services into these pathways and remove potential barriers to student success. For instance, colleges were asked to develop stronger advising systems to help students choose and enter an appropriate program of study, and to modify developmental education courses so that students could advance more quickly into college-level courses. Drawing on analysis conducted by CCRC (Jenkins & Cho, 2012), CBD leaders believed that presenting students with a clear description of what courses students needed to take—and in what sequence—would help students avoid costly mistakes such as taking courses that do not count toward a degree. They identified eight core principles and asked all the colleges to commit to these principles, while giving them flexibility in implementation:

1. Accelerate entry into coherent programs of study
2. Minimize time to get college ready
3. Ensure students know the requirements to succeed
4. Customize and contextualize instruction
5. Integrate student supports with instruction
6. Continually monitor student progress and proactively provide feedback
7. Reward behaviors that contribute to completion
8. Leverage technology to improve learning and program delivery

CBD's Early Implementation Experiences.   MDRC studied the first two phases of CBD by conducting site visits to five colleges in 2013–2014 and administering a survey to approximately 1,500 administrators, faculty, and staff in 2014 (MDRC, 2015). The CBD evaluation did not assess changes in student outcomes across the colleges. Rather, participating colleges were expected to set targets for student performance and monitor their progress on several key indicators, such as the percentage of students completing developmental education requirements by the end of their first year in college and the percentage of students persisting in college between their first and second year.

Because CBD aspired to large-scale changes in institutional practices, the evaluation focused on two dimensions of systemic reform: (a) changes in beliefs and practices of college personnel that were consistent with CBD principles and (b) changes in student experiences. On the first dimension, the MDRC survey found that the attitudes of college administrators, faculty, and staff were generally neutral, with most personnel neither strongly in favor of nor opposed to the CBD reforms. Attitudes did not differ by college, though they did differ by position held at the colleges. Perhaps not surprisingly, the most favorable attitudes toward CBD were held by those who identified themselves as CBD leaders, followed by college administrators. Faculty members were more likely to be neutral or slightly negative, primarily owing to concerns that CBD's goal of helping students progress through college more quickly could lead to some erosion of educational standards or threaten their autonomy as instructors. CBD leaders responded by involving more faculty in planning committees and delegating responsibilities to create more "champions" (MDRC, 2015).

With regard to the second dimension—changes in student experiences—MDRC focused primarily on the implementation of pathway principles by the colleges. The evaluators found some variation across the colleges, but observed that three principles were widely shared: (a) restructuring the sequence and delivery of developmental education classes, (b) streamlining and making more explicit the course sequences needed for their academic programs, and (c) improving academic advising systems. The evaluators also found that colleges placed more emphasis on less expensive reforms, such as encouraging students to choose a program of study early in their college career, rather than on more costly reforms such as enhanced academic advising. Finally, they found a common pattern of implementation at the colleges was running a small pilot before scaling it. Although this may seem counter to the CBD philosophy, the pilots were affordable and provided opportunities for colleges to identify and resolve implementation problems before going to scale. College leaders also noted that they could use the results from successful pilots to generate broader support for particular reforms among skeptical faculty and staff (MDRC, 2015). These findings should be considered preliminary, as implementation was ongoing when the MDRC study was completed.

The CBD experience, like ATD's, underscores that comprehensive reform in community colleges requires sustained effort and attention over many years. It also suggests that an incremental approach—starting with small pilots, and gradually expanding over time—may not be incompatible with comprehensive reform if it helps build support for new ways of doing business and fosters a culture of continuous improvement. The Gates Foundation is not planning a summative evaluation of CBD's effects on student outcomes across the participating states or institutions. Rather, as the initiative enters its scaling phase, it is documenting and communicating implementation lessons that can help inform other colleges across the country on lessons the CBD colleges learned and how to put them into practice.

The Role of Research in Comprehensive Reform Efforts

The experiences of ATD and CBD suggest lessons for strengthening the role of research and evaluation to advance comprehensive community college reform efforts. We consider four phases of comprehensive reform—exploration, implementation, pilot testing, and institutionalization—and what approaches to gathering evidence may be most beneficial in each phase.

Exploration.   In the exploration phase, college practitioners may start by diagnosing problem areas and developing hypotheses about what is causing the problems. Colleges can begin this work by analyzing student records. ATD's five-step improvement process—including its emphasis on longitudinal analysis and identification of achievement gaps between different subgroups—offers one model; CBD's loss and momentum framework is another. Many colleges employ institutional researchers who conduct such analyses. The ATD and CBD experiences underscore the value of involving college administrators and faculty in the research process to pose questions, look for patterns, and generate ideas on how to improve.

Implementation.   During the implementation phase, colleges will shift their focus to understanding the new policies and programs they have put in place. Once again, institutional researchers can work with college administrators and faculty to determine whether new policies or programs are operating as intended and how they might be strengthened. A combination of quantitative and qualitative research methods can shed light on these issues. For example, colleges can use descriptive statistics to document the characteristics of students who participate in an intervention and the percentage of students who complete a course, persist to the next semester, or achieve other outcomes. CBD's key performance indicators provide a useful template for such monitoring. Colleges may also glean insights from focus groups and interviews with faculty, staff, and students to elicit their views on what is working well and what needs improvement.

Pilot Testing.   In the pilot-testing phase of reform, colleges will want to know whether a new policy or program produces intended results. Merely tracking the outcomes of students who participate in a reform is not sufficient, because such indicators alone cannot demonstrate the "value added" of a reform over business as usual. The effectiveness of a reform is most convincingly established by showing that students who experience it have better outcomes than they would have without the reform. Simple comparisons can be deceiving, unless researchers take steps to ensure the equivalence of the comparison group to the group experiencing the reform. Some institutional researchers have the capacity to execute such designs, though it may be useful for colleges to partner with external researchers who have expertise in such methods and who can lend objectivity to the analysis.

The most accurate and reliable means of assessing effectiveness is to use a lottery-like research design in which some students are randomly assigned to a program group that experiences the reform or to a control group that experiences business as usual. When executed properly, random assignment helps ensure that students in the program and control groups start out with similar observable characteristics (such as age and prior years of education) as well as characteristics that may be harder to measure (such as motivation). By tracking both groups over time and comparing their outcomes, researchers can determine whether students in the program group experience better outcomes. Random assignment is not suitable for every program, but it can be a powerful learning tool when the effectiveness of an intervention is truly not known and when more students are eligible for a new policy or program than can be served. Indeed, when program capacity is limited, a lottery is often the fairest strategy to determine who receives an intervention and who does not. The U.S. Department of Education recently issued a free guide and software to help schools and colleges conduct such studies (Schochet, 2015).

Institutionalization.   The final phase of comprehensive reform, institutionalization, may be achieved after a college moves through each of the three preceding phases. Institutionalization occurs when a reform strategy affects all or nearly all students. By definition, researchers cannot construct a comparison group within the same college when all students are affected, so evaluation becomes more challenging. One possible solution is for researchers to track student outcomes at multiple time points to see if significant changes occur before and after the reform is introduced, and to compare these outcomes with patterns observed at other colleges during the same time period. If the colleges that have institutionalized a reform show significant improvement—and if the other colleges do not—this may indicate that the institutionalized reform had a positive effect, though there is a risk that comparison colleges may differ in ways that are not measured, even when they appear to be similar. A stronger design is to randomly assign some colleges to implement the reform and other colleges to continue with business as usual, to ensure that two groups of colleges are equivalent at the start of the study. There are examples in K–12 in which entire schools or school districts have been randomly assigned to program and control groups (Quint et al., 2014; Slavin, Cheung, Holmes, Madden, & Chamberlain, 2013), but no study of this kind has been completed at community colleges.

Lessons Learned

The ATD and CBD initiatives demonstrate the value of research and evaluation in identifying potential obstacles to student success and developing reforms. The initiatives also demonstrate the utility of a systematic approach to data collection and analysis to facilitate learning within and across colleges. It is worth underscoring that research and evaluation alone are not enough to transform an institution and improve student outcomes on a large scale. Colleges must first have a clear understanding of the problems they are trying to solve and invest the time and resources needed for implementing changes. ATD and CBD suggest that progress is often made in small steps, even when there is dedicated effort by college leadership.

Encouragingly, community colleges have made significant advances in identifying policies and practices in need of improvement and are becoming increasingly skilled at using research and evaluation to support the improvement process. By themselves, colleges probably cannot undertake rigorous evaluations of comprehensive, institution-wide reforms, but there is much they can do to assess implementation and to pilot-test the effectiveness of particular interventions. For example, colleges can monitor participation data for new programs they develop to see if they are reaching the neediest students and to ensure that students are attending regularly. If there are limited slots for a new program, colleges can use a lottery to assign students to program and control groups in order to learn whether the program leads to improved outcomes over business-as-usual. When colleges commit to such efforts, they not only gain feedback on their own programs but help build the field's knowledge about what it takes to help students to succeed—and what the elements of an effective, comprehensive reform strategy may look like.

References

Bill & Melinda Gates Foundation. (2010). *Completion by Design concept paper*. Seattle, WA: Bill & Melinda Gates Foundation.

Jenkins, D., & Cho, S.-W. (2012). *Get with the program: Accelerating community college students' entry into and completion of programs of study*. New York, NY: Community College Research Center.

Mayer, A., Cerna, O., Cullinan, D., Fong, K., Rutschow, E.Z., & Jenkins, D. (2014). *Moving ahead with institutional change: Lessons from the first round of Achieving the Dream community colleges*. New York, NY: MDRC.

MDRC. (2015). *Changing community colleges: Early lessons from Completion by Design*. Seattle, WA: Bill & Melinda Gates Foundation.

Quint, J. C., Balu, R., DeLaurentis, M., Rappaport, S., Smith, T. J., & Zhu, P. (2014). *The Success for All model of school reform: Interim findings from the Investing in Innovation (i3) scale-up*. New York, NY: MDRC.

Rutschow, E. Z., Richburg-Hayes, L., Brock, T., Orr, G., Cerna, O., Cullinan, D., ... Martin, K. (2011). *Turning the tide: Five years of Achieving the Dream in community colleges*. New York, NY: MDRC and Community College Research Center.

Schochet, P. Z. (2015). *Statistical theory for the RCT-YES software: Design-based causal inference for RCTs (NCEE 2015–4011)*. Washington, DC: U.S. Department of Education, Institute of Education Sciences, National Center for Education Evaluation and Regional Assistance, Analytic Technical Assistance and Development.

Slavin, R. E., Cheung, A., Holmes, G., Madden, N. A., & Chamberlain, A. (2013). Effects of a data-driven district reform model on state assessment outcomes. *American Educational Research Journal, 50*(2), 371–396.

THOMAS BROCK serves as commissioner for the National Center for Education Research in the U.S. Department of Education's Institute of Education Sciences.

ALEXANDER K. MAYER is senior research associate at MDRC.

ELIZABETH ZACHRY RUTSCHOW is senior research associate at MDRC.

NEW DIRECTIONS FOR COMMUNITY COLLEGES • DOI: 10.1002/cc

3

This chapter describes the structure and implementation of a redesign of developmental education in the Virginia Community College System, discusses preliminary descriptive findings from an evaluation of the redesign, and shares lessons for the field.

The Redesign of Developmental Education in Virginia

Nikki Edgecombe

Developmental education reforms must, by definition, focus on students' early college careers. Perhaps as a result, past efforts have not generated large and enduring positive effects (Cho, Kopko, Jenkins, & Jaggars, 2012; Edgecombe, Jaggars, Baker, & Bailey, 2013; Edgecombe, Jaggars, Xu, & Barragan, 2014; Visher, Weiss, Weissman, Rudd, & Wathington, 2012). Consistent with initiatives like Achieving the Dream that defined student success as college completion and prioritized using data to diagnose and address the obstacles to it, the field has recognized the limitations of developmental education-only reforms and begun integrating developmental education reforms into more comprehensive improvement initiatives. The City University of New York's Accelerated Study in Associate Program (ASAP) is one example. This reform provided a constellation of sustained services, including intensive advising and financial assistance, and showed a nearly twofold increase in 3-year graduation rates for full-time developmental education students (Scrivener et al., 2015).

The Virginia Community College System's (VCCS) statewide redesign of developmental education is noteworthy in its scale and breadth, even though the reform is not as comprehensive as ASAP. In 2008, the VCCS, comprised of 23 community colleges and enrolling more than 262,000 students in 2014–2015, initiated a systemwide developmental education redesign to increase student success, defined primarily as credential completion and transfer. This chapter provides an overview of the developmental education redesign planning and early implementation of the redesign and presents preliminary descriptive findings on its outcomes (Kalamkarian, Raufman, & Edgecombe [2015] describe the redesign). It aligns the redesign with the four phases of comprehensive reform evaluation

New Directions for Community Colleges, no. 176, Winter 2016 © 2016 Wiley Periodicals, Inc.
Published online in Wiley Online Library (wileyonlinelibrary.com) • DOI: 10.1002/cc.20220

discussed in Brock, Mayer, and Rutschow, Chapter 2 of this volume, and highlights considerations for systems pursuing comprehensive efforts to more effectively assess and remediate academic underpreparedness.

Phase I: Exploration

The VCCS saw developmental education redesign as a critical component in improving student success. Similar to the diagnosis process described in the exploration phase by Brock and colleagues in Chapter 2, system office personnel and external research partners conducted data analyses showing that the majority of VCCS students referred to developmental education did not complete it. These findings justified the need for reform and illustrated the vulnerabilities of the existing multisemester developmental education course sequences. The VCCS established the Developmental Education Task Force to review VCCS outcome data and examine national reform approaches. From this research, it articulated three goals that shaped reform planning, design, and implementation: (a) reduce the need for developmental education; (b) design developmental education in a way that reduces the time to complete developmental English and mathematics to one academic year for most students; and (c) increase the number of developmental education students graduating or transferring in 4 years. Only the third goal specified target metrics. For that goal, the task force aimed to increase 4-year graduation and transfer rates from 25% to at least 33%.

Task force members believed that effective implementation would require buy-in at the colleges and gathered input from faculty and administrators who worked most closely with developmental education students to garner broad support for the reform. They then created committees to translate the task force's recommendations into developmental math courses, developmental English courses, and new assessment and placement instruments and policies.

Developmental Math.   The redesign modified developmental math from a sequence of full-semester courses that covered a range of topics to nine shorter sequential modules, each of which covers a limited number of concepts. This change enabled students to test out of discrete modules by demonstrating proficiency on the new diagnostic placement exam and aligned developmental math requirements with students' chosen programs of study. For example, liberal arts majors must complete or place out of modules 1 to 5 in preparation for liberal arts college math. Science, technology, engineering, and math (STEM) majors must complete or place out of modules 1 to 9 to enroll in higher level algebra and precalculus.

The developmental math modules are offered through two course structures. The first is one-credit courses that typically run for 4 weeks, allowing students to take multiple modules per semester. The second is shell courses, which facilitate efficient registration because their length depends on the number of modules (not which modules) a student intends to complete. They allow colleges to group students at different levels and with different module completion requirements in the same course section. Four-credit shell courses typically last 16 weeks and students are required to complete four modules to pass the course. Three-credit shell courses are typically 12 weeks and students must complete three modules to pass.

The VCCS encouraged colleges to integrate technology as part of the redesign. Most one-credit developmental math courses are lecture based and use instructional technology (such as Pearson's MyMathLab) for homework and sometimes for assessments. The majority of shell courses have a computer-mediated instructional delivery model that uses instructional software as the primary means of content delivery, practice, and assessment in the classroom. In these classes, faculty typically circulate and provide one-on-one support to students who could be completing different modules.

Developmental English.   The redesign integrated developmental English and reading and changed course structures to tiered, variable credit, one-semester courses. Students enroll in the redesigned courses based on their placement results. Students assessed at the lowest levels of reading and writing proficiency enroll in an eight-credit integrated developmental English and reading course. Students assessed at a higher level of reading and writing proficiency, but still substantially short of college ready, enroll in a four-credit course. Students assessed modestly below college ready enroll in a two-credit course as a corequisite with college English. The eight- and four-credit courses are designed as direct, one-semester pathways to college English, allowing students to complete developmental and gatekeeper English in 1 year.

Assessment and Placement.   Prior to the redesign, the VCCS used ACT's branded Compass test and statewide cut scores to determine placement in developmental education. The redesign developed new customized assessment and placement systems to improve course placement accuracy, standardized policies systemwide, and introduced performance floors— minimum levels of demonstrated proficiency in math and English— referring students not reaching the floor to adult basic education or other basic skills remediation alternatives.

The math redesign included changes to the assessment instrument and placement policies, with students no longer having to complete the equivalent of intermediate algebra to be eligible to enroll in liberal arts college math courses. The new Virginia Placement Test–Math consists of computer adaptive and diagnostic components. Students who do not show proficiency on the first computer adaptive test, which addresses arithmetic and introductory algebra skills, are directed to a series of diagnostic tests for modules 1 to 5. Students who do not show proficiency on the second computer adaptive test, which assesses intermediate algebra skills, are directed to a series of diagnostic tests for modules 6 to 9. Students who successfully complete

NEW DIRECTIONS FOR COMMUNITY COLLEGES • DOI: 10.1002/cc

the first and second computer adaptive tests qualify to enroll in precalculus and will take an additional test to assess their preparedness for calculus.

The English redesign left placement policy essentially unchanged but significantly modified the assessment instrument to include an essay component. The new Virginia Placement Test–English was designed to assess students' writing, reading comprehension, grammar, vocabulary, and research skills. The computer-based, written essay portion assesses students on organization, focus, development and support, vocabulary, and sentence structure and mechanics. It is graded by the computer using artificial intelligence algorithms. The 40-item multiple choice portion assesses a range of reading and writing fundamentals skills.

Phase II: Implementation

The redesign of developmental math and English was implemented at scale in spring 2012 and spring 2013. Implementation relied on a structured planning process and incorporated elements of Brock and colleagues' implementation phase to assess whether the redesign was operating as intended (Chapter 2). Local implementation benefitted from the staggered rollout of the math and then English, because lessons learned from the math planning and launch could pave the way for English. At the recommendation of the VCCS, most colleges created math and English implementation teams to oversee their planning and rollout. Teams were led by implementation "leads" and typically included senior academic and student services administrators, department chairs, faculty, advisors, admissions and records personnel, and testing center staff. Some colleges also engaged representatives from financial aid, facilities, and academic support services (like tutoring center staff).

The teams' redesign planning work helped identify college functions— beyond developmental math and English classes—that would be affected by the changes. For example, academic advisors had to be trained on how to interpret new placement test results and to properly advise new and returning students into developmental education classes. Team leads often provided advisor training and created informational resources, such as a crosswalk to transition students previously enrolled in developmental education into the appropriate new courses.

Implementation teams were well positioned to address some early, unanticipated consequences of the redesign. For instance, when the first new 4-week, one-credit developmental math course ended, course registration problems arose for students who did not successfully complete module requirements. They had to drop their second, third, and fourth session modules and reenroll in a new module sequence starting with the module they did not complete. This "add-drop-swap" process was labor intensive and required colleges to redeploy staff to verify module completion and to promptly reach out to students needing schedule changes. It also affected the forecasting of enrollment in subsequent one-credit developmental math course sections. In response, implementation teams across colleges shared student information system programming designed to automate grade uploads and decrease the administrative workload. One college created a predictive model to more accurately forecast enrollment in their one-credit courses.

Phase III: Pilot Testing

The VCCS prioritized formative, not summative assessment during the first semesters of redesign implementation, departing from the pilot-testing evaluation phase discussed by Brock and colleagues in Chapter 2. It created internal vehicles to gather and disseminate information on implementation and partnered with external researchers to examine implementation and early outcomes. Because all colleges implemented the redesign at the same time and fully scaled, neither internal nor external evaluation could randomly assign students to program (redesign) and control (business-as-usual) groups as recommended by Brock and colleagues in Chapter 2. Nevertheless, the formative assessment activities and preliminary descriptive outcomes provided information the VCCS used to strengthen implementation.

Internal Monitoring.   The VCCS recognized that colleges wanted information on implementation but faced challenges in obtaining and analyzing it. In response, it established math and English support teams to assess early implementation of the developmental redesigns before any outcomes could be measured. The Developmental Math Implementation Support Team (DMIST) was staffed by college math and science faculty, a former Virginia Department of Education official (for the K–12 perspective), and officials from the VCCS. Members of DMIST visited each community college to examine implementation processes, challenges, and promising practices. They also tried to identify resources the VCCS could provide to support the continuous improvement of the developmental math redesign. The Redesign Implementation Support for English (RISE) consisted of English and math faculty and VCCS officials. The RISE team collected information about the developmental English redesign during its first semester of implementation through visits to a sample of colleges and the administration of online faculty surveys. Both teams prepared reports on early implementation challenges and successes that were disseminated across the VCCS.

The VCCS Office of Institutional Effectiveness tracked and analyzed early outcome data on placement, developmental course completion, and gatekeeper course success in both math and English. In late 2014, it published an evaluation of the redesign that presented short-term descriptive outcomes tied to the redesign goals (VCCS, 2014). The report cited lower developmental education course enrollments, higher gatekeeper math and

English course completion rates, and increased college-level credit accrual relative to periods before the redesign.

External Evaluation.   Although rigorous evidence on whether the developmental education redesign improved student outcomes is not yet available, descriptive analyses of early outcomes conducted by the Community College Research Center, in partnership with the VCCS, suggest that fewer students placed into developmental education and more students enrolled in and successfully completed college math and English courses after the redesign (Kalamkarian et al., 2015; Rodriguez, 2014).

Descriptive analyses of placement rates indicate fewer VCCS students are being referred to developmental math and English since the new placement tests and policies went into effect. Prior to the reform in fall 2010, 83% of first-time-in-college students placed into developmental math and 57% placed into developmental English. Those percentages declined to 57% in math (in fall 2012) and 42% in English (in fall 2013) after the redesign.

Similar analyses of college math and English course enrollment and completion show that 29% of post-redesign college-math-placed students (in fall 2012) enrolled in college math within 1 year compared to 11% of pre-redesign college-math-placed students (in fall 2010). Eighteen percent of college-math-placed students in the post-redesign cohort completed a college math course with a grade of C or higher compared to 8% of college-math-placed students in the pre-redesign cohort. Among students directly referred to college English in fall 2013 and 2010, 52% (post-redesign) and 36% (pre-redesign), respectively, enrolled in college English within 1 year; 39% (post-redesign) and 27% (pre-redesign), respectively, successfully completed the course. The pool of students eligible to enroll in college English upon entry increased after the redesign due to the statewide implementation of a corequisite course model, in which the highest level of developmental English is paired with college English. Including this group of corequisite eligible students, a total of 50% of post-redesign enrollees successfully completed college English in 1 year, a nearly 70% improvement over pre-redesign outcomes.

Phase IV: Institutionalization

The VCCS redesign was implemented at scale from the outset, accelerating the institutionalization phase described by Brock and colleagues in Chapter 2. All 23 community colleges implemented the new developmental math and English assessment and placement system and courses, and all new and continuing developmental education students were affected by the redesign. Although this approach made the type of rigorous evaluation discussed by Brock and colleagues in Chapter 2 more challenging, it presented opportunities as well. Full-scale implementation assured the VCCS that colleges could not functionally opt out of the redesign by implementing small pilots that served only a few students. It also meant that early analyses of outcomes would not be impaired by scaling differences across colleges. At individual colleges, full-scale implementation helped show the full magnitude of unintended consequences (such as the developmental math "add-drop-swap" problem) so that colleges could adequately address them. Although challenges emerged during early implementation, institutionalization did not preclude ongoing refinement. Rather, by necessity in many instances, it supported rapid improvement cycles designed to tap collective expertise to enhance implementation (Bryk, Gomez, & Grunow, 2010).

Lessons Learned: Virginia Redesign as Comprehensive Reform

The VCCS is a pioneer in statewide developmental education redesign, pursuing a simultaneous overhaul of developmental assessment, placement, and courses. As a first-mover, the VCCS and its member colleges created reform development processes that other states or colleges may want to adopt and adapt (Edgecombe, Cormier, Bickerstaff, & Barragan, 2013). They have identified and, in many cases, addressed unforeseen implementation challenges that will likely be encountered by other colleges, used early formative assessment to help develop implementation supports and share best practices among colleges, and examined the early effectiveness of the redesign. These system- and college-level actions occurred as the redesign was implemented at full scale from the start, which accelerated institutionalization.

Given the nationwide call to dramatically improve the outcomes of students referred to developmental education, the VCCS redesign provides at least three important lessons for the field.

First, inclusive, transparent, and well-structured planning at both the system and college levels is crucial to the success of large-scale reform efforts. The VCCS convened a practitioner-led task force to use research to identify how developmental education might have challenged student success in the past. The task force created research-based goals and design principles to guide redesign and inform the activities of statewide committees on developmental math and English coursework, and assessment and placement. Concurrently, colleges created multifunction implementation teams responsible for translating the statewide policies and recommendations to college-level policy and practice. Although this inclusive reform planning approach did not eliminate all redesign implementation challenges, it did help create a coherent vision of the reform and develop state- and college-level infrastructure to support planning, early implementation, and refinement.

Second, operationalization of reforms at the college level varies considerably, suggesting the need for robust implementation supports early on. The Virginia community colleges confronted myriad challenges as they translated the redesign policy into practice, including issues with classroom space, students' course registrations, and forecasting demand for course sections. Because colleges relied on their implementation teams to address these emergent issues, they could develop fixes. For example, one college developed a reliable model to forecast demand for developmental math course sections by analyzing historical data on students' progression patterns after the first semester of implementation. The VCCS also deployed implementation resources based on information gathered from the DMIST and RISE teams, which assessed and supported early implementation. Among the resources coming out of DMIST, for example, was a series of written briefs describing home-grown solutions to common implementation challenges.

Finally, developmental education reforms with greater opportunities for college course enrollment must be integrated into other comprehensive reform efforts to significantly improve college completion. Many students assigned to developmental education could successfully complete college courses (Scott-Clayton, Crosta, & Belfield, 2014). Reforms, like the VCCS redesign, that attempt to determine the students that could complete and create opportunities for them to pursue college-level coursework show early promise in improving short-term outcomes. But prior research also suggests this improvement is not powerful enough to significantly increase college completion on its own (Cho et al., 2012). Therefore, the VCCS took steps to strategically combine reforms to developmental education with other high-impact academic and nonacademic supports that are sustained throughout students' college careers.

This chapter illustrated how expansive interventions such as the VCCS developmental education redesign are important building blocks of comprehensive reform. Each individual building block must be thoughtfully designed and carefully implemented and evaluated. Each must also explicitly connect with other comprehensive reform elements in order to drive dramatically better student outcomes. For the VCCS, the redesign was part of a broader student success strategy. Within this strategy, the redesign focused on addressing high developmental education referral rates and low completion rates. Other VCCS reforms—mandatory success courses, early alert systems, program streamlining, among others—are also underway, each with their own discrete goals but seeking to work in concert with the redesign. Such integration is a key to successful comprehensive reform and a model for the field.

References

Bryk, A. S., Gomez, L. M., & Grunow A. (2010). *Getting ideas into action: Building networked improvement communities in education*. Stanford, CA: Carnegie Foundation for the Advancement of Teaching.

Cho, S. W., Kopko, E., Jenkins, D., & Jaggars, S. S. (2012). *New evidence of success for community college remedial English students: Tracking the outcomes of students in the Accelerated Learning Program (ALP)* (CCRC Working Paper No. 53). New York, NY: Columbia University, Teachers College, Community College Research Center.

Edgecombe, N., Cormier, M. S., Bickerstaff, S., & Barragan, M. (2013). *Strengthening developmental education reforms: Evidence on implementation efforts from the Scaling Innovation project* (CCRC Working Paper No. 61). New York, NY: Columbia University, Teachers College, Community College Research Center.

Edgecombe, N., Jaggars, S. S., Baker, E. D., & Bailey, T. (2013). *Acceleration through a holistic support model: An implementation and outcomes analysis of FastStart@CCD.* New York, NY: Columbia University, Teachers College, Community College Research Center.

Edgecombe, N., Jaggars, S., Xu, D., & Barragan, M. (2014). *Accelerating the integrated instruction of developmental reading and writing at Chabot College* (CCRC Working Paper No. 71). New York, NY: Columbia University, Teachers College, Community College Research Center.

Kalamkarian, H. S., Raufman, J., & Edgecombe, N. (2015). *Statewide developmental education reform: Early implementation in Virginia and North Carolina* (CCRC Research Report). New York, NY: Columbia University, Teachers College, Community College Research Center.

Rodriguez, O. (2014). *Increasing access to college-level math: Early outcomes using the Virginia Placement Test* (CCRC Research Brief No. 58). New York, NY: Columbia University, Teachers College, Community College Research Center.

Scott-Clayton, J., Crosta, P. M., & Belfield, C. R. (2014). Improving the targeting of treatment: Evidence from college remediation. *Educational Evaluation and Policy Analysis, 36*(3), 371–393.

Scrivener, S., Weiss, M. J., Ratledge, A., Rudd, T., Sommo, C., & Fresques, H. (2015). *Doubling graduation rates: Three-year effects of CUNY's Accelerated Study in Associate Programs (ASAP) for developmental education students.* New York, NY: MDRC.

VCCS Office of Institutional Research & Effectiveness. (2014, December 11). *Initial review of the impact of the developmental education redesign at Virginia's Community Colleges.* Richmond, VA: Author.

Visher, M., Weiss, M. J., Weissman, E., Rudd, T., & Wathington, H. (with Teres, J., & Fong, K.). (2012). *The effects of learning communities for students in developmental education: A synthesis of findings from six community colleges.* New York, NY: MDRC.

NIKKI EDGECOMBE *is a senior research associate at the Community College Research Center at Teachers College, Columbia University.*

NEW DIRECTIONS FOR COMMUNITY COLLEGES • DOI: 10.1002/cc

4

This chapter examines the Early Assessment Program, which provides California high school students with early signals about their college readiness and allows them to improve their skills and reduce the need for developmental education in college.

Addressing College Readiness Gaps at the College Door

Elizabeth Friedmann, Michal Kurlaender, Alice van Ommeren

Almost 75% of students enter California's community colleges unprepared for college-level work (California Community College Chancellor's Office, 2015a). Although the need for developmental education in college is not unique to California, its early attempt to boost college preparation in high school is. The state's Early Assessment Program (EAP) provides California high school students with early signals about their college readiness. These signals allow students to improve their skills during their senior year of high school with the goal of reducing the need for developmental coursetaking in college (Achieve, 2010). The EAP program started as a statewide effort initiated by the California State University (CSU) system in 2004 to better align K–12 with the state's less selective 4-year public postsecondary system to reduce the need for developmental education among CSU students. In 2008, the EAP was extended to the California Community College (CCC) system.

This chapter explores the EAP program's adoption and implementation at the CCC. It offers an analysis of the differences in campus adoption of the EAP and assessment rates and developmental coursetaking across California's community colleges before and after the EAP's adoption and addresses the question, "Did any meaningful differences in developmental assessment rates and coursetaking follow the EAP's adoption at CCC?"

Planning for Reform

California's 1965 Master Plan defined unique missions for each of its three public higher education segments to ensure access to postsecondary schooling for all students. The state's top eighth of high school graduates is eligible

NEW DIRECTIONS FOR COMMUNITY COLLEGES, no. 176, Winter 2016 © 2016 Wiley Periodicals, Inc.
Published online in Wiley Online Library (wileyonlinelibrary.com) • DOI: 10.1002/cc.20221

to attend the University of California (UC) and the top third is eligible to attend the CSU. The remainder is served by the CCC system. Community colleges are primarily charged with providing access to three populations: high school graduates not enrolled in the UC and CSU systems but striving for a bachelor's degree; students in pursuit of a vocational or career-technical degree; and adults seeking basic skills, including English as a second language. In 2014, the CCC system served over 2.1 million students per year across its 113 campuses (CCC Chancellor's Office, 2015b). Over 30% of UC graduates and over 50% of CSU graduates begin their postsecondary education at a CCC (CCC Chancellor's Office, 2015b). The success of such CCC students is not enjoyed by all, however. Over 70% of students who begin at college-level work earn a degree or transfer within 6 years of entry, compared to only 40% who arrive in need of some developmental education (CCC Chancellor's Office, 2015b).

In 2007, the California state legislature created the Basic Skills Initiative to address the lack of college readiness among California students and provided supplemental funding for improving outcomes for students needing developmental education. The bill required the CCC Chancellor's Office to create a developmental education evaluation framework and produce an annual accountability report on the system's developmental education needs and offerings. In response, the CCC Chancellor's Office issued the Basic Skills Accountability Report, which tracks the outcomes of students enrolled in developmental coursework.

Concurrent with the push toward improving college readiness, in September 2008, Governor Schwarzenegger signed Senate Bill 946, which extended the EAP to the CCC. Adoption of the EAP is voluntary. Campuses that adopt it apply high school assessment scores as an evaluation of a student's college preparation, thereby potentially reducing the need for additional assessment once the student enters college. The CCC Chancellor's Office provided a variety of incentives to encourage campuses to adopt the high school exam results, including public outreach efforts and grants. Some campuses received financial support to assess high school student data from schools within their district boundaries to better understand college readiness gaps among sending high schools. By 2012, 26 campuses had received microgrants for such outreach, professional development, and coordination efforts (CCC Chancellor's Office, 2012). As a result, EAP take-up rates and timing of adoption varied considerably across the state's CCC campuses.

Reform Efforts: California's Early Assessment Program

The EAP set three goals to spur comprehensive change in the way students prepare for college and in the way K–12 and postsecondary systems could be better aligned. The first goal is to identify students' level of college preparedness while they are still enrolled in high school. Specifically, the EAP was implemented as an assessment in English language arts and mathematics of California 11th-grade students in conjunction with the state's regular assessments for accountability under No Child Left Behind. Although the EAP assessments are voluntary, the vast majority of high schools, and between 80 and 90% of students they serve, participated in 2012 (California State University, 2012). In 2014, California's Common Core State Standards began requiring the EAP as a component of 11th-grade assessments.

The EAP's second goal is to prompt students to improve college readiness during their senior year of high school. To accomplish this goal, students who participated in the EAP exams receive a letter with their assessment results in the spring before their senior year. The letter is meant to provide a signal about their level of college readiness. If students score above a certain threshold, they are "exempt" from taking a placement assessment once they enter the CSU or CCC. If students do not meet this threshold, they are "not exempt" and receive counseling on additional high school coursework and preparation they can take during their senior year to improve their college readiness. Students on the border may be "conditionally exempt" and directed to take specific coursework in their senior year and achieve a satisfactory grade to meet exemption requirements.

The EAP's third goal is to provide better information and training about college-level skills and expectations to high school teachers. Specifically, the CSU designed professional development training for high school English language arts teachers of expository reading and writing. Moreover, the training offers a companion curriculum that high schools could adopt as part of 12th-grade reform of English courses.

Research evaluating the EAP found positive effects. Its adoption reduced developmental coursetaking rates for first-time freshmen by 2 to 3 percentage points throughout the statewide CSU system (Kurlaender, Grodsky, Howell, & Jackson, 2014). The use of and exposure to the EAP expository reading and writing curricula was associated with improved college readiness for students and improved understanding of the writing and reading skills necessary for college among teachers (Fleming, Grisham, Katz, & Suess, 2005; Fong, Finkelstein, Jaeger, Diaz, & Broek, 2015). In addition, CCC students who scored exempt on the EAP seemed to have improved college outcomes. Those scoring exempt in either math or English were more likely to enroll in courses transferable to the CSU or UC, and those scoring exempt in English were less likely to enroll in noncredit bearing courses (Kurlaender, 2014). Still, some researchers argue that the information the EAP provides is too limited or too late to affect student behavior and boost college preparation (Tierney & Garcia, 2011).

Perhaps because of some prodding and incentives by the CCC Chancellor's Office, the number of campuses accepting the EAP in assessing college readiness increased over time. In 2008, the first year after the legislation authorizing the EAP was passed, 24 campuses adopted the EAP. In the second year, an additional 22 campuses adopted it, followed by 21 campuses in

2011, six campuses in 2012, three campuses in 2013, and 1 campus in 2014. As of 2015, 78 campuses had accepted the EAP. This staged adoption allows us to examine how early-adopting campuses differed from later adopters and use this variation in timing of adoption to assess whether adoption of the EAP was followed by reduction in developmental assessment rates and coursetaking.

Investigating Campus Differences in Assessment Rates and Coursetaking

We use a unique administrative data set made available by the CCC Chancellor's Office to assess whether any meaningful differences in developmental assessment rates and coursetaking might have followed the introduction of the EAP. The data are the census of CCC students and include student enrollment data (units attempted and earned, course credit and transfer status and grades), a rich set of student characteristics (race/ethnicity, gender, and financial aid receipt), and faculty and college characteristics (including number of employees and share of faculty designated as temporary). We limit our analytic sample to cohorts of first-time students ages 17–19 in the years 2006–2013 who enrolled in at least six units in their first term. Analysis was restricted to the 109 campuses that opened before 2008.

We investigate campus differences in assessment rates and coursetaking in three different ways. We first examine differences in campus characteristics by timing of EAP adoption. Both campuses and their students have different characteristics, including (among other characteristics) enrollment, number of employees, share of students receiving a Pell Grant, and share of temporary faculty. Because some characteristics vary between campuses, we can explore associations between characteristics and EAP adoption. If differences exist among campuses adopting the EAP and those not adopting it, it might be possible for administrators to identify which campuses might require more intensive discussions in adopting alternative assessment procedures.

Next, we investigate whether (and when) adopting the EAP might have been associated with campus-level rates of developmental education assessments and coursetaking. Campuses that adopted the EAP use assessment scores to evaluate a student's college preparation, which reduces the need for additional assessment once the student enters college. In this analysis, we compare the proportion of first-time students taking any developmental English assessment in their first year at campuses that adopted the EAP to campuses that did not adopt it. We adjusted for a time trend before and after EAP adoption by averaging assessment rates for 2 years before and 2 years after EAP adoption. We can estimate the effects only for campuses that adopted in 2009 and 2010 because not enough years have passed after implementation to assess any effects in campuses adopting the EAP in later years. We analyze only English assessment rates because math EAP had stricter eligibility rules (students must be enrolled in at least algebra II in 11th grade to participate in the math EAP), and CCC math assessments were used for placement into math courses beyond developmental courses. Kurlaender (2014) estimates that only 6% of CCC students who took the math EAP earned exemption status, which suggests math assessments might not decline as a result of the EAP.

Finally, we examine the proportion of students taking any developmental education course in their first year at campuses that adopted the EAP in 2009 and 2010. We limit the analysis to 3 years before and after EAP adoption. Given the positive program effects identified at CSU (see Kurlaender et al., 2014), we might expect rates of developmental coursetaking to decline after the EAP program was expanded to the CCC system. Although very few students enrolling at the community colleges received an exempt score on the EAP (Kurlaender, 2014), the information provided to students not designated as exempt on the EAP may have motivated them to use their senior year to prepare for college, which could help all campuses enroll better prepared students, regardless of whether they accept the EAP.

When interpreting results of these analyses, it is important to note that CCC campuses differed in their administration of developmental courses in several critical ways. Most important, they used different assessments to determine the need for developmental English and math coursework. Other differences include the cutoffs chosen to determine college readiness, criteria applied to course placements (such as high school grades), enforcement of cutoffs and alternative options (i.e., some opt for more self-placement), and availability of developmental education courses. Although such differences make it difficult to assess systemwide EAP reform efforts, we can compare students' course behavior in precollege level courses before and after reform efforts at each college.

The comparison of campus-level outcomes before and after adoption of the EAP does not account for trends over time that are not associated with the introduction of the EAP (for example, changes in the types of students enrolling). However, we use a technique called "difference in differences" (DID) to better isolate the unique changes that could have occurred with adoption of the EAP. The intuition behind this approach is that all campuses may have experienced changes during this time period in addition to EAP adoption. If we compare changes in campuses that adopted the EAP with changes in campuses that did not, the DID allows us to identify whether the changes of those that adopted the EAP differed in a unique way from those who did not, and to control for a variety of campus-level characteristics that could affect college differences in both adoption of the EAP and in outcomes. To further control for factors that could affect changes in developmental coursetaking over time, both across the entire system and by campus EAP adoption, we use a time-series analysis to investigate whether the introduction of the EAP at CCC altered the trajectory of assessments and developmental coursetaking for adopting campuses.

NEW DIRECTIONS FOR COMMUNITY COLLEGES • DOI: 10.1002/cc

Findings

Results of our three analyses—examinations of characteristics of early and late adopters, changes in the rates of developmental education course-taking, and changes in the proportion of students taking developmental coursework—allow us to answer the research question "Did any meaningful differences in developmental assessment rates and coursetaking follow the EAP's adoption?" We address each in turn.

Characteristics of Adopters.   We see distinct differences in characteristics in campuses that were early adopters of the EAP (implemented the EAP prior to 2011), late adopters (implemented in 2011 or later), and nonadopters by 2014. For example, the 45 early-adopting and the 30 late-adopting campuses were significantly larger than the nonadopting campuses, having over 1,000 more students enrolled on average, and averaged more employees and faculty designated as temporary. Systemwide, average student enrollment in 2008 was 15,700 but ranged at the campus level from under 2,000 to over 38,000 students. Early-adopting campuses also averaged about 75% part-time students, compared to 73% systemwide. No significant differences in campus EAP adoption existed by race/ethnicity levels or by the proportion of Pell recipients.

Changes in Assessment Rates.   Most campuses experienced a reduction in the share of first-time students taking an English assessment in their first year between 2008 and 2013 and results from the DID analyses show no statistically significant effect of EAP adoption on English assessment rates. Why are we not seeing any direct effect of the EAP on developmental assessment rates? One reason might be that very few high school students who took the EAP and enrolled at a community college received an exempt status score on the EAP. Of the 72,312 community college students who took the English EAP in 2009, only 13% scored exempt (Kurlaender, 2014). As a result, it is unlikely that the EAP would dramatically alter the need for further assessments once students enrolled at community college. Still, the signal about college readiness (more often than not as "not ready") may have led to better performance on those assessments and reduced the need for developmental coursework, an outcome we evaluate next.

Developmental Coursetaking.   Compared to campuses that had not adopted the EAP by 2014, we estimate that English developmental course-taking rates at early-adopting campuses declined by about 6 percentage points between 2006 and 2013 (from an initial 71% in 2006). Results for developmental math coursetaking are similar. At early-adopting campuses, developmental math coursetaking rates declined by about 6 percentage points (from an initial 71% in 2006), relative to nonadopting campuses. All declines are statistically significant, even after controlling for a variety of campus-level factors (total enrollment, share of Hispanic students, share of Pell recipients, share of part-time students, number of employees, and share of faculty designated as temporary).

Lessons Learned

State policy makers and administrators of statewide community college systems can use lessons from the voluntarily adoption of EAP to help build college readiness among the students they serve. First, campus characteristics might determine which campuses adopt an early assessment tool. Our analysis suggests that larger campuses might be more inclined to adopt an early assessment tool. If size reflects organizational capacity, state-level policy makers and administrators might want to ensure capacity in their campuses prior to implementing an early assessment tool.

Second, the low rates of CCC students scoring exempt on the English portion of the EAP suggest that the state's comprehensive reform efforts should better align K–12 and postsecondary systems to reduce deep deficiencies in college readiness that emerged at the 11th grade. In addition to improved standards in K–12 (currently being implemented through Common Core), the state might also require a stronger and earlier signal to students.

Finally, early assessment programs might both positively influence high schools and their students to better prepare for college or prompt CCC campuses to reconsider how they assess and place students in developmental courses. Although the significant declines in developmental coursetaking patterns in CCC, both systemwide and in campuses that implemented the EAP, were not necessarily *caused* by the EAP or by campus decisions to adopt it per se, the reduction in developmental coursetaking across the CCC may have been associated with it: declines were larger at campuses that adopted the EAP.

California state reforms seeking to reduce the need for developmental education have been in effect for over a decade. The EAP, which assesses college readiness during high school, seems to have been associated with reductions in developmental coursetaking across the CCC in recent years and is now part of California's Common Core State Standards. The observed reductions in developmental coursetaking across the CCC are likely a combination of the true impact of EAP and broader efforts at the CCC to address the high rates of developmental coursetaking. Even so, California's experience with EAP shows how comprehensive reform in community colleges may extend beyond the campuses themselves to improve student outcomes systemwide.

References

Achieve. (2010). *Strategies for K–12 and postsecondary alignment.* Washington, DC: Author.

California Community College Chancellor's Office. (2012). *Program update: Early Assessment Program.* Sacramento, CA: Author. Retrieved from http://extranet.cccco.edu/Portals/1/SSSP/EAP/Resources/CCCEAPUpdate2012-01-27.pdf

California Community College Chancellor's Office. (2015a). *Key facts.* Sacramento, CA: Author. Retrieved from http://www.californiacommunitycolleges.cccco.edu/PolicyInAction/KeyFacts.aspx

California Community College Chancellor's Office. (2015b). *Early Assessment Program.* Sacramento, CA: Author. Retrieved from http://californiacommunitycolleges.cccco.edu/Portals/0/FlipBooks/2015_Early_Assessment_Program/2015_EAPReport_ADA.pdf

California State University. (2012). *Early Assessment Program (EAP) for college readiness.* Long Beach, CA: Office of the Chancellor, California State University System. Retrieved from http://eap2012.ets.org/

Fleming, D., Grisham, D., Katz, M., & Suess, E. (2005). *Pilot study evaluation of the Early Assessment Program's professional development in English 2004–05.* Long Beach, CA: Office of the Chancellor, California State University System.

Fong, A., Finkelstein, N., Jaeger, L., Diaz, R., & Broek, M. (2015). *Evaluation of the Expository Reading and Writing Course: Findings from the Investing in Innovation Development Grant.* San Francisco, CA: WestEd.

Kurlaender, M. (2014). Assessing the promise of California's Early Assessment Program for community colleges. *Annals of the American Academy of Political and Social Science, 655*(1), 36–55.

Kurlaender, M., Grodsky, E., Howell, J., & Jackson, J. (2014). *Ready or not? California's Early Assessment Program and the transition to college.* Working Paper.

Tierney, W., & Garcia, L. (2011). Remediation in higher education: The role of information. *American Behavioral Scientist, 55*(102), 102–120.

ELIZABETH FRIEDMANN *is a doctoral candidate in School Organization and Education Policy at the University of California, Davis.*

MICHAL KURLAENDER *is professor of education at the University of California, Davis.*

ALICE VAN OMMEREN *is dean of research, analysis and accountability at the California Community Colleges Chancellor's Office.*

NEW DIRECTIONS FOR COMMUNITY COLLEGES • DOI: 10.1002/cc

5

This chapter examines the use of technology and other structural changes to encourage comprehensive advising reforms.

Transforming the Community College Student Experience Through Comprehensive, Technology-Mediated Advising

Shanna Smith Jaggars, Melinda Mechur Karp

Navigating college is complicated. As Scott-Clayton (2011) points out, incoming community college students must choose whether to attend college full time or part time; consider an array of potential programs, majors, and transfer options; and choose from a long menu of courses. Qualitative evidence from community colleges suggests that the complexity of academic decision making results in student mistakes, such as graduating with "excess credits" or earning credits that do not transfer to a student's chosen 4-year destination (Bailey, Jaggars, & Jenkins, 2015).

To help guide students through the landscape of program and course options, all colleges provide academic advising services; unfortunately, most community colleges can fund only one advisor for every 800 to 1,200 students (Karp, 2013). To provide the sustained, extensive, and personalized support that is necessary (Karp & Stacey, 2013), colleges would need to substantially increase their number of academic advisors. Given increasing enrollments and decreasing public allocations, community colleges need more cost-effective solutions.

In this chapter, we examine strategies to help transform academic advising to provide sustained, personalized support within the resource constraints faced by community colleges. We first describe typical community college intake and advising processes and a vision for transforming them. As an initial step toward this transformation, many community colleges are adopting "e-advising" technologies that they hope will allow them to deploy scarce advising resources more efficiently and effectively. Using case study data gathered from several community colleges engaged in technology-mediated advising reforms, we suggest that e-advising tools may be most

New Directions for Community Colleges, no. 176, Winter 2016 © 2016 Wiley Periodicals, Inc.
Published online in Wiley Online Library (wileyonlinelibrary.com) • DOI: 10.1002/cc.20222

effective when they prompt colleges to rethink and restructure delivery of an array of services and programs into a more cohesive and intentional whole.

Advising at a Typical Community College

Due to high numbers of students who must be processed within the few weeks prior to a new semester, initial advising meetings at a typical community college may be as short as 10 or 15 minutes (Grubb, 2006; Jaggars & Fletcher, 2014). Within this short time frame, advisors review the student's developmental education placement test scores and create a suggested course schedule for the first semester based on those placements (Bailey et al., 2015). Typically there is no time for an in-depth discussion of the student's interests and strengths, potential transfer schools, career planning, or how the student might embark on an exploration of those issues. Although students who have already decided on their program of study may be pleased with such a speedy and efficient meeting, those who are undecided often feel confused and frustrated and may want advisors to take more time to understand their individual situation and tailor a set of courses to their needs (Jaggars & Fletcher, 2014). To create a more supportive advising system without substantially increasing costs, community colleges have increasingly adopted three interconnected strategies in the past decade: enhanced advising for academically vulnerable students, online advising information provision, and student success courses.

Enhanced Advising.   Ideally, academic advisors help students explore their skills and interests, investigate various occupational and professional career paths that may match those interests, and create a coherent plan for academic and career progress (Gordon, 2006; Holland, 1997). Across the span of the student's time in college, the advisor may continue to help the student reexamine goals and reformulate a plan to meet those goals.

At most community colleges, academic advisors are far too overburdened to provide such intensive and ongoing advising to all students. However, many colleges provide "enhanced" advising programs, including mandatory meetings, an assigned advisor for each student, and longer advising sessions, to small, specific populations deemed to be particularly at risk. Rigorous studies of enhanced advising suggest that this approach has positive impacts on student performance and retention (Bettinger & Baker, 2014; Scrivener et al., 2015; Weiss, Brock, Sommo, Rudd, & Turner, 2011). These studies also find that more-intensive models (such as a mentor who reaches out to assigned students regularly to discuss priorities, identify academic and nonacademic barriers, and create plans to overcome those barriers) have stronger and longer term impacts than less-intensive approaches to enhanced advising. The sustained effects of the more-intensive models may be due to their focus on helping students develop self-reflection and planning skills, which allows them to more successfully self-advise in subsequent terms.

Online Information Provision.   In the absence of personalized assistance, many students turn to the college website to understand the programs available, whether a potential program is a good fit for them, and the steps necessary to complete the credential. Ideally, the website should provide detailed information about each program, allowing students to answer questions such as: How long does the program take to complete, and which specific courses are required? What are graduates' typical occupations and entry-level wages? Do articulation agreements with nearby colleges guarantee graduates junior-level standing in a related major? Unfortunately, most colleges' websites do not feature such detailed and clear information, and even when such information is available, many students have difficulty interpreting and applying it without assistance from an advisor (Jaggars & Fletcher, 2014; Margolin, Miller, & Rosenbaum, 2013; Van Noy, Weiss, Jenkins, Barnett, & Wachen, 2012).

Student Success Courses.   One approach to providing students with more sustained advising is the student success course, also known as College 101 or Introduction to College. These courses, offered in most colleges around the country, provide students with information about campus and basic success skills. Research shows generally positive outcomes for students (for example, Cho & Karp, 2013; Schnell & Doetkott, 2003). However, these effects tend to fade over time (Rutschow, Cullinan, & Welbeck, 2012; Weiss et al., 2011), suggesting that student success courses may need additional refinement if they are to promote sustained student success.

Qualitative research provides one possible explanation for this fade-out effect (Karp et al., 2012; O'Gara, Karp, & Hughes, 2009). In-depth examination of student success courses at three colleges found that they typically cover a wide range of content in a short period, leading to teacher-directed, lecture-based pedagogies focused on "covering all the topics" rather than on fostering deep learning (Karp et al., 2012). As a result, student success courses effectively deliver important information for students but may not help students develop the ability to use their newfound knowledge in future courses.

A Vision for Transformation

Enhanced advising for small subsets of students, online information provision, and student success courses are all good steps forward, but even when applied together, they are insufficient to meet students' needs. Drawing from ongoing innovations and research in the field, researchers and practitioners are beginning to understand that student support services require a more significant transformation, which some colleges are beginning to implement through three additional and interrelated strategies: simplifying program and transfer structures, more explicitly teaching students how to self-advise, and leveraging online "e-advising" tools to make advisors' work more in-depth, effective, and efficient.

New Directions for Community Colleges • DOI: 10.1002/cc

Simplifying Program and Transfer Structures.   Students would not need as much advising if their choices were less complex. For example, some community colleges offer highly structured career-technical programs, including a very specific sequence of courses to be taken in lockstep with a peer cohort (Van Noy et al., 2012). After making the decision to enter such highly structured programs, students have no need for further advising in course selection: all students take the same courses together throughout the remainder of the program. However, such a lockstep approach is not feasible for most students (Bailey et al., 2015). A majority arrive on campus undecided on their program of study and need time to explore their options; moreover, transfer-oriented students need flexibility in course selection to meet the requirements of their particular transfer destination. Other students need flexibility to balance school and family or work obligations.

To provide an optimal balance between clear-cut structures and flexible opportunities for exploration, practitioners and researchers are increasingly interested in the "guided pathways" model (Bailey et al., 2015). In this model, students who have chosen a major or program are provided with a program map that defines a default sequence of courses, which are aligned with requirements for successful transfer or career advancement. New students who are undecided about a major are required to choose one of a limited number of exploratory or "metamajors" that expose them to educational, career, and transfer options within a broad field (such as business, health, or liberal arts). The metamajors also include program maps of default sequences of courses, with the first semester's courses providing a foundation applicable to any major within the metamajor. The program map strategy not only eases students' course selection decisions, but also makes it possible for advisors to track progress and intervene if students are not making headway or straying "off-map."

Teaching Students How to Self-Advise.   Some students are more adept at self-advising than others. For example, a recent study gave students information and asked them to respond to advising scenarios (Jaggars & Fletcher, 2014). A handful of students earned nearly perfect scores, whereas other students attempting the same scenarios with the same resources were unable to find and apply the appropriate information.

Self-advising is a skill, and similar to any other skill, it is one that could be taught by the college. To teach students self-advising skills without substantially increasing advising staff, colleges might consider mandating an orientation for incoming students to expose them to available online tools and provide practice in using them. Beyond that initial exposure, however, students need ongoing practice in how to identify their interests, sift through and interpret related information, set long-term goals, and plan out steps toward those goals. This type of practice could be built into a mandatory first-semester student success course focused on building the metacognitive skills students need to effectively self-advise. More broadly, colleges may also need to consider how their general education curriculum can incorporate instruction and practice in how to find, interpret, weigh, and apply information to make decisions.

Leveraging More Sophisticated E-Advising Systems. A growing array of e-advising products may help colleges improve and expand the online component of their advising services. In particular, tracking or early alert systems can help colleges identify students who are struggling in key courses within their major, who are enrolling in courses inappropriate to their major, or who are demonstrating poor attendance or academic performance. By identifying struggling students early, colleges can intervene before small problems become insurmountable. These systems can also help streamline case management and information-sharing across college personnel.

E-advising systems can also encourage "triaging," in which colleges determine which students' advising needs can be handled through automated systems, versus which students require intensive face-to-face advising. For example, recent research finds that students value independent engagement with technology for relatively straightforward advising functions, but value one-on-one interaction for more complicated decision making (Kalamkarian & Karp, 2015).

E-advising systems may allow colleges to "do more with less" by using advisors' time more efficiently and effectively. To reach this goal, however, advisors and other staff may need to do their jobs differently. For example, triaging enables some students to bypass advising centers in favor of self-advising, thereby freeing up advisors to spend more time with students with more profound needs. But such a change requires advisors to rethink how they help some students learn to self-advise, as well as how they work with other students in a more long-term, in-depth, and developmental manner.

Barriers to Successful Advising Transformation

Like any comprehensive reform, colleges engaging in the types of transformative advising change described here and throughout this volume encounter multiple challenges. Advising reforms are particularly difficult because they require both structural changes (for example, revised programs of study) and changes in how advisors perform their everyday work tasks. The Community College Research Center (CCRC) recently studied six colleges engaging in technology-enabled advising reforms ("Integrated Planning and Advising Services," referred to as IPAS), in which we examined the colleges' redesign, implementation, and roll-out processes. Importantly, although IPAS reforms included a technological component, they also included other pieces of advising redesign, such as encouraging program planning or launching early warning systems.

Over the course of 18 months, CCRC interviewed faculty, staff, and students to understand their attitudes toward, experiences with, and changed practices resulting from IPAS implementation. Next, we discuss a number of challenges observed as these six colleges sought to transform advising.

Colleges Focused on Technical Rather than Adaptive Change.   Technical change involves straightforward problems with known answers; adaptive change involves unclear problems, or problems with unknown solutions (Heifetz, 1994). Getting e-advising products up and running is a technical change. Although the challenges involved are often time consuming, they can be surmounted through knowledge-gathering and clear-cut problem solving. In contrast, the transformation of advising is an adaptive change: no specific solutions exist for how to restructure student support services, especially within the resource constraints that often face community college advising departments. For example, there are no obvious ways to ensure that advisors use e-advising products once available, nor that college faculty will adopt metamajors and simplified program structures.

When organizations or groups confront adaptive problems, they often switch their focus to technical issues, as these are more easily solvable and do not require hard conversations about unspoken assumptions (Heifetz, 1994). Similarly, the colleges in our study tended to focus on the technical aspects of reform, such as deploying e-advising systems, rather than the adaptive aspects, such as changing advisors' work. As a result, although all of these colleges implemented IPAS systems, after 18 months, few saw meaningful changes in how advisors actually did their work or how students were supported. Although focusing on the technology seems like an obvious first step, it may be wasted if it is not conducted in parallel with the more challenging work of figuring out what to do with the technology once it is deployed.

Colleges Lacked a Clear Vision.   Comprehensive reform requires a clear vision of benefits—an actionable and shared image of what the reform will look like in practice and why it will address key problems (Karp & Fletcher, 2014). A clear vision helps stakeholders understand what they will be expected to do once the reform is complete and why. A vision also helps stakeholders focus on the adaptive changes described previously, by providing a framework for thinking about norms, behaviors, and assumptions that contribute to changed practices.

Colleges in our study had a broad sense of what they wanted their reform to accomplish, but this vision often lacked specificity. For example, a college may have wanted their reform to reduce complexity and improve students' advising experiences but could not articulate how the reform would accomplish those goals. It is difficult for advisors to meet a vague goal such as "improve students' experiences." When they are provided with a clear vision, such as "meet every semester with a cohort of students to help them plan their long-term programs, and connect them to community resources that address out-of-school challenges," advisors can understand what is expected of them and shift their practices accordingly.

NEW DIRECTIONS FOR COMMUNITY COLLEGES • DOI: 10.1002/cc

We also found that some colleges had multiple competing visions between stakeholders. For example, at one institution, the college leadership viewed advising reforms as a way to create holistic support for students, whereas project leadership viewed them as an attempt to create efficiencies and make their work lives easier. Without a shared vision, colleges struggled to translate their reform into changed practice. Advisors lacked clear guideposts and so continued to do their jobs as they always had.

Colleges Encountered Challenges with Triaging.   Colleges in the study were enthusiastic about the potential of e-advising technologies to help triage students; however, they struggled to answer a number of challenging questions. For example, at what point in the semester should faculty be encouraged to identify and flag struggling students? Perhaps 3 weeks into the semester is too early for faculty to accurately identify who is struggling; yet if it is much later, students may not have time to recover from early stumbles. If a student is flagged, how should the intervention be handled, how often should the student be contacted, and what type of message would be most effective?

Colleges were also overwhelmed by triaging information and lacked processes to address the needs of identified students. For example, one college instituted an IPAS system that made it easier for faculty to raise flags when students struggled. The system worked: faculty raised thousands of flags in the first semester of system activation. All of these flags, however, were sent to a single individual who was unable to sort through them, identify which were most urgent, and direct students to appropriate supports in a timely manner.

In general, triaging is useful only if identified students can be subsequently supported. Some colleges lacked a robust set of student services. In these colleges, identifying struggling students was only minimally helpful, because there was no way to meaningfully intervene and provide them with help once they were identified as needing support. To free resources to support some students more intensively, advisors and faculty had to allow other students to self-advise using online resources—a strategy that raised an additional set of challenges.

Some Students Resisted Self-Advising.   Some students at the six colleges were enthusiastic about self-advising, many others were not. Some students preferred in-person advising because they did not know how to self-advise, a problem that could be addressed through an orientation or student success course. Many students needed help wading through complexity, a problem that could be addressed by streamlining programs. For others, however, the "personal" touch was important: some may have faced unique challenges that required the creative problem-solving power of an expert, and some may have felt a degree of anxiety that could be allayed only through the reassurance of human contact.

Students were most amenable to self-advising when engaged in activities that were administrative in nature, such as registering for classes.

They also were open to technology as a way to receive encouragement and support from college personnel, for example, via email. However, for in-depth advising activities, such as deciding on a major or creating a long-term plan, students preferred to meet in person (Kalamkarian & Karp, 2015).

Lessons Learned

Of the six colleges in our study, several moved their IPAS reforms forward. Their experiences provide lessons for other colleges seeking to engage in transformative advising reform.

Engage in a Long-Term Planning Process. The colleges that made the greatest progress also spent substantial upfront time planning for new processes and structures, engaging cross-functional and cross-hierarchical stakeholders in the visioning process. They thought deeply about their current student support mechanisms, what they hoped to accomplish, and how current processes would change. For example, one college documented students' experiences from recruitment through graduation and designed reforms to address service gaps and major loss points. Rather than selecting strategies from externally defined "best practices" or based on the newest technology, they focused on what advisors and other personnel would need to do to better support students and then selected strategies and technologies that would help them achieve those specific goals.

Regard Technology as a Means, Not an End. The most successful colleges thought about structures, not products: they designed their reform first and identified the technology later. By focusing on broader reforms, rather than on technology per se, colleges pushed themselves to confront and address adaptive challenges. This approach also enabled colleges to be more nimble. In contrast, colleges that started with a product and designed a reform around it tended to feel constrained by the limits of what the product could do.

Simplify. Simplification reduces student confusion and the need for advising. Some colleges simplified advising structures, for example, with one-stop shops or assigned case managers. Some colleges simplified curricula, thereby moving closer to the broader and more comprehensive reform known as "guided pathways" (Bailey et al., 2015).

Teach Students to Self-Advise. Although students often resist self-advising, in some colleges, staff also resisted it because they did not believe students had the metacognitive or organizational skills to self-advise. To help teach students these skills, a number of colleges implemented, revised, or were considering student success courses to focus on self-advising. Such courses may be particularly effective when they give students the opportunity to practice skills such as program planning as part of the curriculum (Karp et al., 2012).

Conclusion

Comprehensive advising reforms often rely heavily on technology, but the technology alone is insufficient. Advisors and faculty must also rethink how they "do business," by simplifying program pathways, designing and implementing case management processes, and teaching students how to self-advise. Although the challenges of transformative reform are steep, they are not insurmountable. By committing to sustained visioning, planning, and ongoing improvement, colleges can achieve the goal of comprehensive support for all students.

References

Bailey, T. R., Jaggars S. S., & Jenkins, D. (2015). *Redesigning America's community colleges: A clearer path to student success*. Cambridge, MA: Harvard University Press.

Bettinger, E. P., & Baker, R. (2014). The effects of student coaching: An evaluation of a randomized experiment in student advising. *Educational Evaluation and Policy Analysis, 36*(1), 3–19.

Cho, S. W., & Karp, M. M. (2013). Student success courses in the community college: Early enrollment and educational outcomes. *Community College Review, 41*(1), 86–103.

Gordon, V. N. (2006). *Career advising: An academic advisor's guide*. San Francisco, CA: Jossey-Bass.

Grubb, W. N. (2006). "Like, what do I do now?": The dilemmas of guidance counseling. In T. Bailey & V. S. Morest (Eds.), *Defending the community college equity agenda* (pp. 195–222). Baltimore, MD: Johns Hopkins University Press.

Heifetz, R. A. (1994). *Leadership without easy answers*. Cambridge, MA: Harvard University Press.

Holland, J. (1997). *Making vocational choices: A theory of vocational personalities and work environments* (3rd ed.). Odessa, FL: Psychological Assessment Resources.

Jaggars, S. S., & Fletcher, J. (2014). *Redesigning the student intake and information provision processes at a large comprehensive community college* (CCRC Working Paper No. 72). New York, NY: Columbia University, Teachers College, Community College Research Center.

Kalamkarian, H. S., & Karp, M. M. (2015). *Student attitudes towards technology-mediated advising systems* (CCRC Working Paper No. 82). New York NY: Columbia University, Teachers College, Community College Research Center.

Karp, M. M. (2013). *Entering a program: Helping students make academic and career decisions* (CCRC Working Paper No. 59). New York, NY: Columbia University, Teachers College, Community College Research Center.

Karp, M. M., Bickerstaff, S., Rucks-Ahidiana, Z., Bork, R. H., Barragan, M., & Edgecombe, N. (2012). *College 101 courses for application and student success* (CCRC Working Paper No. 49). New York, NY: Columbia University, Teachers College, Community College Research Center.

Karp, M. M., & Fletcher, J. (2014). *Adopting new technologies for student success: A readiness framework*. New York, NY: Columbia University, Teachers College, Community College Research Center.

Karp, M. M., & Stacey, G. W. (2013). *What we know about non-academic supports*. New York, NY: Columbia University, Teachers College, Community College Research Center.

Margolin, J., Miller, S. R., & Rosenbaum, J. E. (2013). The community college website as virtual adviser: A usability study. *Community College Review, 41*(1), 44–62.

O'Gara, L., Karp, M. M., & Hughes, K. L. (2009). Student success courses in the community college: An exploratory study of student perspectives. *Community College Review, 36*(3), 195–218.

Rutschow, E. Z., Cullinan, D., & Welbeck, R. (2012). *Keeping students on course: An impact study of a student success course at Guilford Technical Community College.* New York, NY: MDRC.

Schnell, C. A., & Doetkott, C. D. (2003). First year seminars produce long-term impact. *Journal of College Student Retention, 4*(4), 377–391.

Scott-Clayton, J. (2011). *The shapeless river: Does a lack of structure inhibit students' progress at community colleges?* (CCRC Working Paper No. 25). New York, NY: Columbia University, Teachers College, Community College Research Center.

Scrivener, S., Weiss, M., Ratledge, A., Rudd, T., Sommo, C., & Fresques, H. (2015). *Doubling graduation rates: Three-year effects of CUNY's Accelerated Studies in Associate Programs (ASAP) for developmental education students.* New York, NY: MDRC.

Van Noy, M., Weiss, M. J., Jenkins, D., Barnett, E. A., & Wachen, J. (2012). *Structure in community college career-technical programs: A qualitative analysis* (CCRC Working Paper No. 50). New York, NY: Columbia University, Teachers College, Community College Research Center.

Weiss, M. J., Brock, T., Sommo, C., Rudd, T., & Turner, M. C. (2011). *Serving community college students on probation: Four-year findings from Chaffey College's Opening Doors program.* New York, NY: MDRC.

SHANNA SMITH JAGGARS *is former assistant director of Community College Research Center and current director of student success research for the Office of Distance Education and E-Learning at The Ohio State University.*

MELINDA MECHUR KARP *is assistant director of the Community College Research Center, Teachers College, Columbia University.*

NEW DIRECTIONS FOR COMMUNITY COLLEGES • DOI: 10.1002/cc

6

This chapter describes career pathways that evolved through a Trade Adjustment Assistance Community College and Career Training consortium grant designed to help students complete programs of study and enter health care careers.

Using Career Pathways to Guide Students Through Programs of Study

Debra D. Bragg, Marianne Krismer

Many students struggle to persist in college. Ambiguous course requirements, inadequate student support services, and weak alignment with employment opportunities leave students wondering whether they should complete their program of study and whether college is a good investment. When the college experience is confusing and frustrating, it is understandable that students drop out. Minority, low-income, and other students historically underrepresented in higher education are the most vulnerable at successfully navigating the complex rules of college (Goldrick-Rab, 2006), which contributes to their high rates of attrition.

This chapter offers insights into the implementation of career pathways based on the experiences of community college practitioners who are reforming health care pathways as part of a Round 1 Trade Adjustment Assistance Community College and Career Training (TAACCCT) grant. It shows how career pathways guide students through logically structured programs of study that lead to enhanced student retention, completion, credentialing, and employment.

What Are Career Pathways?

Career pathways provide guidance and support to enter, navigate, and complete college so the end goal of securing employment is always in sight. They provide clearly structured programs of study offering contextualized academic instruction that is integrated with career-technical education and with academic and career services that intentionally support student success. They are closely aligned to industry sectors and living-wage job opportunities. The sequenced curricula in these pathways support completing

New Directions for Community Colleges, no. 176, Winter 2016 © 2016 Wiley Periodicals, Inc.
Published online in Wiley Online Library (wileyonlinelibrary.com) • DOI: 10.1002/cc.20223

a program of study and industry-recognized credentials that serve as a stepping-stone to progressively more advanced postsecondary study, additional credentials, and career advancement (Jenkins, 2006; Kozumplik, Nyborg, Garcia, Cantu, & Larsen, 2011). Students who successfully participate in career pathways are prepared to meet occupational requirements associated with their chosen careers. Because job progression is often not linear, but a series of movements between jobs and organizations (U.S. Department of Labor, n.d.-b), career pathways also can prepare students for climbing career ladders and navigating the career lattices that define the group of related jobs that comprise a career.

When combined into a cohesive collection of academic- and student-centered strategies, career pathways can provide students with what Rosenbaum, Deil-Amen, and Person (2006) call the *package deal* that students need to succeed in college and prepare for productive careers. The package deal of reforms associated with career pathways varies to accommodate the needs of diverse students, but often includes the following six elements.

Career-Focused Curriculum and Instruction.   Since the 1980s, colleges have been encouraged to integrate career-technical education and academic education and avoid tracking students into short-term job training that offers limited career growth (Bragg, 2012). Career pathways represent a solution to this problem because they support a "vertically and horizontally integrated system of workforce training that stretches from noncredit adult education through the baccalaureate" (Jacobs & Dougherty, 2006, p. 60). In this way, career-focused curriculum and instruction may break down the silos between career-technical education and transfer education by recognizing that most postsecondary curricula are intended to lead to credentials with currency in higher education and the workplace (McCarthy, 2015).

Competency-Based Core Curriculum.   Because they focus on students' demonstration of clearly defined and measurable learning outcomes, competency-based curricula may be especially appropriate for adult learners, allowing them to apply knowledge and skills gained through experience and supporting acceleration toward credentials (Klein-Collins, 2012; Person & Thibeault, Chapter 8 of this volume). Moreover, competency-based models typically link curricular content to knowledge and skills required for jobs, which helps ensure that program content is relevant beyond the classroom (Ganzglass, Bird, & Prince, 2011), potentially encouraging students to complete and increasing their chances of obtaining employment when they do.

Stackable Credentials.   Stackable credentials are part of a sequence of credentials that can be accumulated over time. Often beginning with entry-level certification and progressing to associate and baccalaureate or higher level degrees, stackable credentials enable career pathways and career ladders to allow college credits to count toward multiple, sequenced credentials.

Intensive Support Services.   Career pathways link students strategically to intensive support services to help them move into and through their program of study. Typically, they accommodate a wide variety of students, use college and career advisors to empower students to contribute to their selecting careers that match their interests and aspirations (Bragg, 2010), and use a student-centered advising approach to help students understand how to navigate their college experiences (Jaggars & Karp, Chapter 5 of this volume).

Accelerated Credit Attainment, Including Credit for Prior Learning.   Career pathways allow working learners to return to higher education throughout their lifetimes offering these students education, career, and social mobility.

Contextualized Developmental Education.   Rather than requiring students to complete developmental sequences (in reading comprehension, writing, or math) prior to entering a program of study, career pathways seek to integrate developmental coursework within the career-technical coursework required for a program of study. This can save students' time and help them apply developmental content in the field in which they ultimately hope to complete a credential (Rutschow & Schneider, 2012).

Promoting Career Pathways in Community Colleges

The Alliance for Quality Career Pathways (AQCP), developed by the Center for Law and Social Policy (CLASP) (2014), offers guidance to assist practitioners in designing and implementing career pathways. Focusing on the state, regional, and local levels, CLASP emphasizes the importance of system change with career pathways at the center of the reform. The Pathways to Results (PTR) initiative (Pickel & Bragg, 2015) drew lessons from AQCP and offers methods for optimizing access and outcomes for diverse learners. These methods include helping practitioners gather and analyze disaggregated data on student subgroup performance to help improve pathways and programs of study for all learners. The primary mission of PTR is to ensure that colleges address inequitable outcomes so all students are positioned favorably to achieve their desired college and career goals.

Many of these practices were codified by the federal government and built into the TAACCCT program. In April 2012, the leaders of the U.S. Departments of Labor, Education, and Health and Human Services endorsed and defined career pathways in a joint letter describing career pathways as:

[A] series of connected education and training strategies and support services that enable individuals to secure industry relevant certification and obtain employment within an occupational area and advance to higher levels of future education and employment in that area. (Dann-Messier, Oates, & Sheldon, 2012, p. 1)

The TAACCCT initiative is consistent with President Obama's calls for community colleges to prepare high-skill workers for a wide range of jobs in all industries to stimulate economic growth. The U.S. Department of Labor (DOL) Solicitation for Grant Applications (SGA) for Round 1 of TAACCCT required that federal funds "create tailored education and training programs to meet employers' needs and give students the skills required to obtain good jobs, earn family-sustaining wages, and advance along a career pathway" (Department of Labor, 2011, p. 3). The TAACCCT vision of career pathways emphasizes programs of study that offer competency-based curricula that prepares students to enter family living-wage employment. The development of "programs of study that meet industry needs, including the development and implementation of career pathways" was one of four TAACCCT Round 1 priorities. By requiring that students enroll in programs of study leading to industry-recognized credentials, TAACCCT linked the federal investment in career pathways to recovery of the U.S. economy.

Building Health Care Career Pathways Through TAACCCT

TAACCCT funds supported pathways in the health care sector, in part, because of its importance to the U.S. economy. During 2015, health care added approximately 470,000 jobs, making it one of the largest and most robust sectors for employment growth (Bureau of Labor Statistics, 2016). The sector's size and continuing importance to an aging population stress the need for career pathways that provide entry and progression in health care jobs.

Cincinnati State Technical and Community College in Cincinnati, Ohio received a Round 1 consortium TAACCCT grant with funding starting on October 1, 2011, to build health care pathways. As the lead college, it led the Health Professions Pathways (H2P) consortium of nine colleges in five states (Ohio, Illinois, Kentucky, Minnesota, and Texas). Because colleges in the consortium represent a diverse set of geographic locations, institutional sizes, and student demographics, they provide an interesting and useful case study for examining career pathways in the health care sector.

To guide the implementation of career pathways, the consortium looked to the past to build support for new health care reform. For example, consortium leaders studied early reports by the Far West Lab (1994) and the Pew Health Professions Commission (1995) to understand how health care education could integrate foundational core curriculum into career pathways within disciplines and career ladders between different health care professional positions and organizations. Common core competencies advanced by the Institute of Medicine (Greiner & Knebel, 2003) and the health care competency framework of the U.S. DOL (n.d.-a) were adopted in the consortium's first year, refined, and subsequently validated by employers in the health care sector. Ultimately, the reform envisioned by the H2P consortium focused on health care pathways as guided by the package deal and consistent with the TAACCCT SGA.

NEW DIRECTIONS FOR COMMUNITY COLLEGES • DOI: 10.1002/cc

Career-Focused Curriculum and Instruction.   The health care core curriculum implemented by the H2P consortium began with a model developed by El Centro College, a member of the consortium. El Centro began developing its core in the mid-1990s, eventually creating six courses: Wellness and Health Promotion, Basic Health Professional Skills, Health Professions Skills 2, Pathophysiology, General Health Professions Management, and Pharmacology. Competencies taught in this core curriculum are crosswalked with the foundational skills assessed by ACT WorkKeys using work-readiness standards, and the DOL's allied health competency model   (www.careeronestop.org/CompetencyModel/competency-models/allied-health.aspx.)

Competency-Based Core Curriculum.   The H2P consortium embraced a competency-based core curriculum as a foundation to all health care pathways, enrolling over 2,000 students in this curriculum. Because career pathways that use competency-based models are complex and necessarily touch many aspects of an institution (Person & Thibeault, Chapter 8 of this volume), the H2P consortium developed a set of design principles that offered guidance on engaging employers and other stakeholders in validating core competencies, developing new credentials and adapting existing credentials to ensure that students can secure entry and progressively advanced employment, engaging community college faculty and administration in addressing the rapidly changing health care landscape, gaining joint ownership and collaborative partnerships with employers and workforce agencies, and using and analyzing data to measure student learning and close gaps in outcomes between diverse student groups.

Stackable Credentials.   The consortium's plans for implementing health care pathways drew on the National Career Cluster Framework (National Association of State Directors of Career Technical Education Consortium, n.d.) to identify and classify the consortium college's 87 programs of study into pathways associated with therapeutic services, diagnostic services, and health informatics that prepare students for entry-level occupations to occupations requiring baccalaureate and higher credentials. For example, the path to a licensed practical nursing (LPN) credential starts with certified nursing assistant and patient care technician certificates, giving LPN graduates the option to progress to the associate degree and the bachelor of science in nursing. Approximately 350 H2P students earned more than one credentials, and another 523 students were still enrolled when the grant ended in September 2015.

Intensive Student Supports.   All nine colleges in the consortium offered student services focused on retaining participants to complete their programs of study and attain credentials. These services focused on outreach, recruitment, and access for underserved students, one-on-one advising delivered when students are in greatest need of direction and support, and nonacademic support services focused on helping students address personal and professional needs. In H2P colleges, the notion of proactive advising extends beyond traditional academic advising, including using grant funds to hire professionals dedicated to providing proactive advising, guidance, and other supports to nearly 4,000 H2P program of study participants (Office of Community College Research and Leadership [OCCRL], 2015).

Accelerated Credit Attainment, Including Credit for Prior Learning. The consortium colleges sought ways to assist students to enter college and quickly find the best fit for their career aspirations in health care. They offered students academic and career assessments, including credit for prior learning. Though most of the H2P consortium colleges had such policies "on the books," the TAACCCT grant supported new policies and processes to provide students with credits to accelerate their progress toward credentials. Across the consortium, 415 students earned at least some credit for prior learning for a total of 3,055 credits, averaging about 7 credits granted or waived per student.

Contextualized Developmental Education. The H2P consortium committed to implementing health care contextualized developmental-level reading, writing, and math. Two colleges offered one semester of contextualized health care-related developmental education courses, and several others offered enhancements to developmental education, including tutoring, supplemental instruction, and boot camps. One college developed an integrated biology and health sciences course that was adopted by numerous programs of study throughout the institution, not only those affiliated with health care programs of study (OCCRL, 2015).

Evaluating and Scaling the H2P Consortium

The H2P consortium closely monitored the implementation and outcomes of career pathways. Formal third-party evaluation of the curriculum provided evidence of how implementation unfolded, including curriculum development, and employer engagement (OCCRL, 2015). The fact that the consortium commissioned a third-party evaluation—which was not a Round 1 grant requirement—demonstrated its commitment to using evidence to build effective career pathways.

Recognizing the career pathway approach requires data to measure performance, colleges in the H2P consortium made substantial enhancements to student, program, and institution-level evaluation systems, consistent with their commitment to using evidence to implement new and improve existing programs of study. Each college hired one or more data managers, built internal relationships between program staff and institutional researchers, increased the capacity of college personnel to assess employment outcomes, and used disaggregated results to study and address performance gaps between student groups.

H2P colleges used the methods recommended by the PTR initiative to improve student outcomes in health care pathways that were not achieving results commensurate with the consortium's performance targets or that demonstrated differences in outcomes between student groups. Its PTR analyses explored the reasons minority and nontraditional students were not represented at expected rates, reasons for financial literacy challenges among low-income learners, and reasons for lagging rates of retention and credential attainment among historically underrepresented groups. Data were used to design and test solutions to close gaps in outcomes among different student groups, and these changes were put into place and evaluated as curriculum change continues to unfold since the TAACCCT grant ended September 2015.

Finally, evaluation results contributed to the H2P consortium's efforts to scale the package deal of health care pathway reforms. The H2P consortium leadership formed a national advisory council with senior-level decision makers from education, industry, accreditors, professional associations, private funders, and workforce agencies. The goal of the consortium to scale health care curriculum reform to 100 community colleges and their workforce partners has made substantial progress, reaching 35 community colleges besides the nine H2P consortium colleges. Other partners, such as the National Network of Health Career Programs in Two-Year Colleges and the Health Professions Network, have signed on to assist with the scaling work. Moreover, a Round 3 TAACCCT grant led by Los Angeles Trade Technical College is involved in scaling activities with other California community colleges through September 2017.

Lessons Learned

Launched through the TAACCCT grant program, the H2P consortium committed to implementing, improving, and scaling health care career pathways that deliver structured curriculum as part of a package deal of reform that enables students to achieve their college and career goals. Four important lessons emerge from their efforts that may enable other community college educators to engage in career pathway reform.

First, the commitment of leaders to organize and support individuals who help create reform is critical to bringing about lasting change, particularly one as extensive as the health care pathways reform associated with H2P. Changes that require restructuring policies, programs, and practices, including creating vertical and horizontal system change, require leaders who are able to help others transition from the old to the new.

Second, career pathway reforms thrive on partnerships and processes that value new ideas from both inside and outside the community college. Community college educators who develop relationships with employers, workforce, and community leaders are positioned to understand how evolving social and economic dynamics need to be addressed by their institutions. These efforts help to ensure what the colleges are teaching and how they are teaching it remains relevant for all students, including students from diverse backgrounds and nontraditional students who work while attending college and advancing in their careers.

Third, putting students at the center of curriculum planning and implementation is critical to meeting their needs. Curriculum reforms, such as the competency-based core curriculum adopted by the H2P consortium, should be accompanied by educators' proactive recruitment of students who have not participated in health care programs in the past. Past lack of broad student participation was not because underrepresented students were not present in the participating colleges' communities; but the consortium colleges recognized the students' absence and built on-ramps to enable them to participate in the reformed programs of study. Practitioners associated with the H2P colleges learned that, when a genuine commitment to access and success is made to all students, especially spotlighting students who have limited or no experience with college, the culture of the community college shifts to a more inclusive, supportive learning environment that is more productive for both students and educators.

Fourth, using data to support changes to curriculum, policy, and practice enhances the sustainability of reform. The H2P consortium committed to building a comprehensive data system that gathered implementation, performance, and impact data that were analyzed, shared, and used to bring about changes as the grant was implemented. This level of engagement with data was unprecedented among the colleges that were part of H2P, even among those engaged in other data-driven reforms such as Achieving the Dream (Brock, Mayer, & Rutschow, Chapter 2 of this volume). The intensive use of data informed educators on students' progression through pathways and increased their appreciation for the ways in which data could be used to reform curriculum and inform the scaling of health care pathway reform to other campuses.

Whereas some might argue that community colleges have always enabled students to link their coursework and credentials to employment, until recently, many community college educators had not considered career pathways as a priority for all students. Educators such as those affiliated with the H2P consortium no longer view career pathways as an option for some, but rather as an opportunity for all. By understanding why students come to college, what assets they bring with them, and how they seek to benefit from both college and career experiences, community colleges can build career pathways that enable all students to succeed. The H2P consortium realized its goal to reform health care education, a goal that continues to drive practitioners affiliated with the member colleges to scale health care pathways reform nationwide.

References

Bragg, D. D. (2010). *Ready for college in Colorado: Evaluation of the Colorado SUN and the college connection program*. Denver, CO: Colorado Community College System.

Retrieved from http://occrl.illinois.edu/files/Projects/colorado_sun/Report/CO_SUN_Final_Eval.pdf

Bragg, D. D. (2012). Career and technical education. In J. Levin & S. Kater (Eds.), *Understanding community colleges* (pp. 187–202). London, England: Routledge/Taylor Francis.

Bureau of Labor Statistics. (2016). Current employment statistics highlights. Washington DC: Author. Retrieved from http://www.bls.gov/web/empsit/ceshighlights.pdf

Center for Law and Social Policy (CLASP). (2014). *Shared vision, strong systems: Alliance for Quality Career Pathways framework*. Washington DC: Author. Retrieved from http://www.clasp.org/resources-and-publications/files/aqcp-framework-version-1-0/AQCP-Framework.pdf

Dann-Messier, B., Oates, J., & Sheldon, G. (2012, April 4). Dear colleague letter highlighting the joint commitment of the U.S. Departments of Education, Health and Human Services, and Labor to promote the use of career pathways approaches. Retrieved from http://www2.ed.gov/about/offices/list/ovae/ten-attachment.pdf

Far West Lab. (1994). *National health care skill standards*. San Francisco, CA: Author. Retrieved from http://files.eric.ed.gov/fulltext/ED377365.pdf

Ganzglass, E., Bird, K., & Prince, H. (2011). Giving credit where credit is due: Creating a competency-based qualifications framework for postsecondary education and training. Washington, DC: Center for Law and Social Policy. Retrieved from http://www.clasp.org/resources-and-publications/files/Giving-Credit.pdf

Goldrick-Rab, S. (2006). Following their every move: How class shapes postsecondary pathways. *Sociology of Education, 79*(1), 61–79.

Greiner, A. C., & Knebel, E. (Eds.). (2003). *Health professions education: A bridge to quality*. Washington, DC: Committee on the Health Professions Education Summit, Institute of Medicine of the National Academies of Science.

Jacobs, J., & Dougherty, K. (2006). The uncertain future of the community college workforce development mission. In B. K. Townsend & K. J. Dougherty (Eds.), *New Directions for Community Colleges: No. 136. Community college missions in the 21st century* (pp. 53–62). San Francisco: Jossey-Bass.

Jenkins, D. (2006, August). *Career pathways: Aligning public resources to support individual and regional economic advancement in the knowledge economy*. New York: Workforce Strategy Center. Retrieved from http://www.workforcestrategy.org/html/publication/62

Klein-Collins, R. (2012). *Competency-based degree programs in the US: Postsecondary credentials for measurable student learning and performance*. Chicago, IL: Council for Adult and Experiential Learning. Retrieved from http://files.eric.ed.gov/fulltext/ED547416.pdf

Kozumplik, R., Nyborg, A., Garcia, D., Cantu, L., & Larsen, C. (2011, September). *Career pathways toolkit: Six key elements of success*. Washington, DC: Social Policy Research Associates. Retrieved from http://www.workforceinfodb.org/PDF/CareerPathwaysToolkit2011.pdf

McCarthy, M. A. (2015). *Flipping the paradigm: Why we need training-based pathways to the bachelor's degree and how to build them*. Washington DC: New America. Retrieved from https://static.newamerica.org/attachments/11652-flipping-the-paradigm/Flipping-the-Paradigm.0f26409a95ec4052987af5d3084d477f.pdf

National Association of State Directors of Career Technical Education Consortium. (n.d.). *Career clusters*. Silver Spring, MD: Author. Retrieved from http://www.careertech.org/sites/default/files/CareerClustersPathways.pdf

Office of Community College Research and Leadership (OCCRL). (2015). *Third party evaluation of the Health Professions Pathways (H2P) consortium: Nine co-grantee college site reports*. Champaign, IL: Author, University of Illinois at Urbana-Champaign.

Pew Health Professions Commission. (1995). *Critical challenges: Revitalizing the health professions for the twenty-first century.* San Francisco, CA: UCSF Center for the Health Professions. Retrieved from http://healthforce.ucsf.edu/publications/critical-challenges-revitalizing-health-professions-twenty-first-century

Pickel, J., & Bragg, D. D. (2015). Pathways to Results: How practitioners address student access, outcomes and equity in an associate degree nursing program. In E. L. Castro (Ed.), *New Directions for Community Colleges: No. 172. Understanding equity in community college practice* (pp. 43–55). San Francisco: Jossey-Bass.

Rosenbaum, J., Deil-Amen, R., & Person, A. E. (2006). *After admission: From college access to college success.* New York: Russell Sage Foundation.

Rutschow, E. Z., & Schneider, E. (2012). *Unlocking the gate: What we know about improving developmental education.* New York: MDRC. Retrieved from http://www.mdrc.org/sites/default/files/full_595.pdf

U.S. Department of Labor. (2011). *Notice of availability of funds and solicitation for grant applications for Trade Adjustment Act Community College and Career Training grant program.* Washington, DC: Author. Retrieved from http://www.doleta.gov/grants/pdf/SGA-DFA-PY-10-03.pdf

U.S. Department of Labor. (n.d.-a). *Allied health competency model.* Washington, DC: Author. Retrieved from http://www.careeronestop.org/competencymodel/competency-models/allied-health.aspx

U.S. Department of Labor. (n.d.-b). *Career ladders and lattices.* Washington, D.C.: Author. Retrieved from http://www.onetcenter.org/ladders.html

DEBRA D. BRAGG *is the director of Community College Research Initiatives at the University of Washington.*

MARIANNE KRISMER *is the national director of the Health Professions Pathways (H2P) Consortium headquartered at Cincinnati State Technical and Community College in Cincinnati, Ohio.*

NEW DIRECTIONS FOR COMMUNITY COLLEGES • DOI: 10.1002/cc

7

This chapter uses Rio Salado College and the Online Education Initiative in the California Community Colleges to illustrate how community colleges can enhance system efficiency and student success in online learning and program completion.

Leveraging Technology to Create a Student-Focused Environment

Linda M. Thor, Joseph Moreau

As the adoption of online education grows, educators grapple with improving online learner retention and successful course completion, which are typically lower than in traditional, face-to-face courses. Institutions that are part of statewide public higher education systems face numerous and significant challenges, such as differing institutional policies and procedures, regulatory restrictions, and local faculty governance, that can make or break initiatives geared toward implementing successful, systemwide, shared online courses, programs, and support services.

The California Community College (CCC) system, through its Online Education Initiative (OEI), is assembling programmatic components for comprehensive reform in an intentional and cohesive network to improve student support and success while enhancing systemwide coordination and collaboration. The $57 million specially funded initiative is available to all 113 community colleges. Its primary goal is to improve student completion and transfer rates by providing robust instructional and support services such as a common course management system, online tutoring, course design standards, a course exchange, student online course readiness support, and professional development for faculty.

The OEI draws on experiences from a very successful online pioneer, Rio Salado College in Tempe, Arizona, to identify best practices that can be scaled. Rio Salado is the largest online community college in the country and uses a "systems approach" to produce fully online, well-defined courses with purposeful learning outcomes and comprehensive and integrated student services. The intentional and cohesive strategy ensures high-quality courses, embedded student services, and effective faculty professional development and support. This marriage of online courses and relevant

NEW DIRECTIONS FOR COMMUNITY COLLEGES, no. 176, Winter 2016 © 2016 Wiley Periodicals, Inc.
Published online in Wiley Online Library (wileyonlinelibrary.com) • DOI: 10.1002/cc.20224

services, supported by sophisticated technology and driven by a systems approach, led to Rio's 68% course completion rate (grade C or better), about 18% higher than the national average, and the highest college graduation rate (in 3 years) among public 2-year colleges in Arizona (Lorenzo, 2012, p. 20).

Rio Salado modeled its approach to online education after Russell Ackoff's view (1994) of systems, where performance depends not only on each part but also on its successful interaction with other parts. Rio Salado's online learning system facilitates organizational learning and performance by sharing data, information, and insights across eight specific functions: course production and support, student enrollment services, faculty services, marketing, online library/media support, faculty and staff development, instructional and technical support, and institutional research. The development team that oversees the system ensures a holistic approach to distance learning that focuses on student success: faculty and representatives from each functional area meet weekly to collaborate and communicate on system-level issues.

This framework enables scalability and consistency that are not available to an individual instructor or program. Rio Salado's online courses follow explicit design standards that are developed by a team of faculty content experts, instructional designers, and technologists, in an approach similar to that taken in the competency-based education outlined by Person and Thibeault in Chapter 8 of this volume. Support services are often available 24/7 and are accessible from within the courses as part of the course management system. Any college service available in person is also available online with faculty and students receiving assistance from both technology and instructional helpdesks.

The systems approach differs from the "craft model" used by most colleges and universities in developing and offering online courses. In the craft model, an individual faculty member structures and designs the course, puts it into the course management system, identifies electronic resources, answers all student questions, addresses proctoring issues, and handles various student needs, such as advising and tutoring. This model limits scalability as only the faculty member who developed the course teaches and supports it. Additionally, the craft model can lead to inconsistent quality and inadequate student and faculty support (Smith & Rhoades, 2006, p. 99).

From a Systems Approach to a Craft Method and Back to the Systems Approach

The CCC system has actively offered distance education courses for almost 50 years. They began with an early systems approach to distance learning but reverted to the craft model, before returning to a systems approach in its current OEI.

Beginning in the late 1960s, broadcast television courses brought educational opportunities to thousands of students without requiring them to leave their homes. In the 1970s, cable television expanded the opportunity to broadcast prerecorded content asynchronously and frequently and, as a result, the penetration and popularity of television courses, or "telecourses," grew. Producing even the most basic telecourse is complex and expensive, which precludes an individual instructor or even an individual college from undertaking the endeavor and makes a systems approach essential. The need for the systems approach strengthened as telecourses evolved from simply broadcasting a faculty member's lecture to elaborately produced video content. Organizations such as Intelecom, Dallas Telecourses, and PBS employed a sophisticated systems approach to content development, involving subject matter experts, instructional designers, professional on-camera talent, and video production specialists.

The rapid infusion of Internet technology into education in the mid-1990s left the telecourse less popular as an instructional delivery method. Often, with a single, low-cost computer, a faculty member could develop extensive, customizable, and personalized content for asynchronous courses with a greater variety in topics than could cost-effectively be addressed by telecourses. Individual faculty members throughout the country embraced the new technology and assumed the role of author, producer, and distributor of distance education content in ways that were rarely possible during the telecourse era. This craft model approach to course development was generally viable and effective when Internet-based or online courses primarily consisted of text, static images, hyperlinks to other Internet sources, and few truly interactive components. However, as technology provided a greater variety of online information sources and opportunities for interactivity, and as students' technological sophistication and expectations for interactivity intensified, the craft model of online course development lost its viability.

During the 2012–2013 academic year, the CCC system offered more than 41,000 online courses to more than 620,000 students, primarily using the craft model. Few colleges in California employed instructional designers, media specialists, accessibility specialists, or information technology staff dedicated to supporting faculty in course content design and development. Although faculty members recognized the need for such support systems and repeatedly requested these resources, it was not until 2013 that California made a significant investment in a systems approach to online instruction. In that year, the state recognized that online education can respond to ebbs and flows of enrollment and state funding better than bricks and mortar education and made a 5-year initial investment in the OEI program. Subsequently, Foothill-De Anza and Butte-Glenn Community College districts were selected to lead the initiative statewide.

The OEI's primary mission is to dramatically increase the number of California community college students who obtain associate degrees and transfer to 4-year colleges each year by providing online courses and services within a statewide online education ecosystem. Its work plans are developing in an integrated fashion similar to how Rio Salado operates, including a common course management system, quality standards, faculty professional development, and comprehensive student services. It engaged with two major research organizations to assess the effectiveness of the project. The Research and Planning Group (www.rpgroup.org), the project's external evaluator, will regularly assess individual program components and advise the project staff on areas targeted for performance improvement. The Public Policy Institute of California (www.ppic.org) will evaluate the impact of the project on statewide metrics such as closing the achievement gap and improving the transfer rate.

Lessons for Moving Online Technologies Forward

The OEI team modeled many of its processes and strategies on the Rio Salado systems model—particularly those strategies that contribute to effective scalability, sustainability, and consistent course quality. The team worked diligently to build on the successes of Rio Salado and adapted its strategy to the complex regulatory environment of the CCC system. For many of the project components, it is too early as of this writing to determine the initiative's impact on student retention and success. Nevertheless, faculty, staff, and administrators throughout the state have enthusiastically accepted the project, which the OEI team believes to be an important precursor for success. The project team also dedicated itself to learning from the experiences of other organizations and systems that have sought to move in this direction in addition to Rio Salado. Campus Computing Project, the Unizin Consortium, MindWires Consulting, the California State University, Hanover Research, the Gates Foundation, and Lumen Learning were among the many colleagues consulted at the beginning of the project.

This research, reinforced by interactions with CCC stakeholders, produced early lessons learned:

- Include faculty significantly and actively in the planning and design process for statewide systems and services. Without a strong faculty voice in the project, failure is nearly certain.
- Communicate, communicate, communicate! A project of this scope has so many moving parts there can seemingly never be enough communication to all stakeholders about decisions, the rationale for those decisions, and the outcome (good or bad) of those decisions.
- Be prepared to be extraordinarily agile. Technology is changing so fast and some of the best opportunities for serving students may appear with little or no notice. Project leaders must be ready and able to change direction wisely and thoughtfully when they identify new and better opportunities to support students, faculty, and staff in an online ecosystem.

NEW DIRECTIONS FOR COMMUNITY COLLEGES • DOI: 10.1002/cc

The California project team has successfully taken a number of significant steps, any of which could have become stumbling blocks without benefiting from the lessons learned by Rio Salado and other early adapters. These steps include:

- Identifying a statewide course management system. OEI identified Instructure's Canvas because the majority of the colleges indicated a desire to migrate to that system over the next 3 years.
- Beginning a pilot project to offer a statewide online tutoring platform and network of professional online tutors. The CCC system selected Link Systems International, Inc. to provide the online tutoring platform at no cost to all colleges. Professional tutors are funded for the OEI pilot colleges, but all colleges may purchase professional tutor services through a statewide contract at a very favorable rate.
- Developing an online course readiness assessment tool and tutorial materials to assist students in navigating and completing online courses. Materials available have extraordinarily high production value and are platform agnostic, making them adaptable to any course management system, portal, or website. OEI is making these materials available to all colleges at no cost.
- Developing online course design standards and a course review process to assist faculty in identifying course design strategies that improve student engagement and assure accessibility. The statewide academic senate endorsed course design standards and course review processes and OEI made them available to all colleges. Faculty from throughout the state have been trained in the standards and processes and OEI compensates them to conduct reviews for their peers.
- Redeveloping an online faculty professional development program to reflect the latest online pedagogies and technologies and to incorporate the prior online teaching experiences of faculty. OEI's new program will streamline faculty development by integrating it with local training opportunities and recognizing the prior experience of faculty.
- Hiring a cadre of instructional designers, accessibility specialists, and other technologists to support faculty in the ongoing development of high-quality online instructional content. Most colleges do not have the staff resources in house to provide the support needed, nor can they necessarily justify the expense. The OEI-provided shared talent pool in these areas is proving to be both useful and sustainable.

Although in 2016, the project is still very much in its infancy, the systems approach to online education, based on the Rio Salado model and scaled to a statewide level, appears to be an exceptional return on investment for the California community colleges and the state of California. Its scale has allowed the project to acquire resources on terms and conditions generally not available to a single institution. For example, the adoption of Canvas as a common course management system is projected to save more than 50% of costs over the current systems licensed by individual colleges. In addition, best practices in online instruction and support can be systemically developed and shared throughout the state more effectively and the student readiness assessment and tutorial material can be developed with a level of production quality not generally achievable by a single college. As such, the cost effectiveness of shared support resources is undeniable. Consequently, the majority of the state's 113 colleges are looking to adopt some or all of the components of the project with a momentum that is unprecedented.

References

Ackoff, R. (1994). *The democratic corporation.* New York, NY: Oxford University Press.

Lorenzo, G. (2012). *A systems approach: Expanding access and achieving student success through support services at Rio Salado College.* Williamsville, NY: The SOURCE on Community College Issues, Trends & Strategies.

Smith, V., & Rhoades, G. (2006, Fall). Community college faculty and web-based classes. *Thought & Action: The NEA Higher Education Journal.* Washington, DC: NEA Communications Services.

LINDA M. THOR *is chancellor emeritus of the Foothill-De Anza Community College District and the former president of Rio Salado College.*

JOSEPH MOREAU *is vice chancellor of the Foothill-De Anza Community College District.*

NEW DIRECTIONS FOR COMMUNITY COLLEGES • DOI: 10.1002/cc

8

This chapter examines how one college implemented a competency-based model to improve student success and transform the way the college creates and maintains career-relevant curricula.

Competency-Based Programs as a Lever for Reforming Core Areas Jointly

Ann E. Person, Nancy Thibeault

In October 2012, under Round 2 of the Trade Adjustment Assistance Community College and Career Training (TAACCCT) grants program, the U.S. Department of Labor (DOL) awarded a $12 million grant to a consortium of three colleges, led by Sinclair Community College (Ohio), to fund a 3-year project titled "Adapting and Adopting Competency-Based IT Instruction to Accelerate Learning for TAA-Eligible, Veterans, and Other Adult Learners." Under the grant, Sinclair and its two cograntees would adapt and adopt the Western Governors University (WGU) model of competency-based education (CBE) in information technology (IT) programs. At Sinclair, the grant-funded "Accelerate IT" program offered credentials in network administration, engineering and security, as well as software development and testing.

This chapter draws on data collected as part of the DOL-mandated third-party evaluation of the Sinclair consortium's TAACCCT grant. Although the evaluation examines experiences at all three partner colleges (Person, Goble, & Bruch, 2014; Person, Goble, Bruch, & Mazeika, 2015), this chapter focuses on Sinclair's use of the grant to advance a vision of comprehensive institutional change. Data sources from the evaluation included program development documents and semistructured telephone and in-person interviews with Sinclair's Accelerate IT program stakeholders that were conducted in mid-2013 and early 2015.

The Path Toward Competency-Based Education

Starting with the proposal development phase, Sinclair leadership viewed the TAACCCT grant in general and the competency-based approach in particular as having transformative potential. They believed the personalized learning approach developed under the grant could drive major changes throughout the institution that would improve student outcomes in a way that could be sustained over time. The CBE approach supports personalized learning by defining precise learning goals and desired competency levels, which are clearly linked to program content; students access the content they need to reach the defined learning goals and competency levels. Moreover, leaders sought to decouple learning from the time constraints of the academic calendar to allow students flexibility in balancing the demands of school, work, and family. The CBE model supports this flexibility by offering courses online with rolling starts throughout the regular academic term, allowing students to move through courses at an accelerated pace.

The TAACCCT grant built on Sinclair's history of leveraging grant funding to support broader institutional improvement. In particular, two National Science Foundation (NSF) grants had laid the foundation for the CBE approach. The first, awarded in 1999, supported the redesign of Sinclair's IT curriculum to align with state and industry standards. The second, awarded in 2003, supported the modularization of IT course content into discreet units linked to clear learning objectives—an important step toward a competency-based approach. More recently, Sinclair's participation in the Bill & Melinda Gates Foundation's Completion by Design initiative (Brock, Mayer, & Rutschow, Chapter 2 of this volume) pushed the institution to undertake comprehensive reform, rethinking its policies and processes and restructuring its academic programs to remove barriers and enhance supports for students to move successfully into and through programs of study. The TAACCCT grant aligned well with this broader vision for change and helped the college further develop and institutionalize the various pieces that one project leader described as an "intentional" path toward CBE. As Bragg and Krismer (Chapter 6 of this volume) explain, the TAACCCT grants program encouraged such comprehensive approaches.

In developing the grant, Sinclair operationalized its approach to comprehensive change in line with the three-pronged definition used in this volume. First, student success motivated and provided the key indicator of success. Specifically, because CBE is student-centered, it has an explicit focus on student learning with an eye to further educational and career outcomes (Johnstone & Soares, 2014). At the same time, the CBE model allows for near constant assessment of student learning through frequent low-stakes assessments to support learning and progress and proctored high-stakes assessments at key junctures ensure competency. Second, the changes Sinclair leaders envisioned under the TAACCCT grant were packaged under a comprehensive theory of institutional change. As articulated in the 2011 grant proposal, the project sought to "revolutionize educational delivery to accelerate credential attainment . . . by translating traditional seat-time based programs into ones in which students earn [credentials] by demonstrating the knowledge, skills, and abilities defined by information technology (IT) employers." Moreover, Sinclair leadership designed the grant with scale, replicability, and sustainability in mind, specifying that partner colleges should build upon the grant-funded models by developing competency-based career pathways in other disciplines and sharing lessons with other colleges. Third, project leaders and Accelerate IT program staff used data from multiple sources to guide program development and improvement. They did this primarily through (a) internal monitoring of enrollment and progress at the student, course, and program levels; (b) DOL performance reporting of key participation and outcome indicators and related benchmarking; and (c) collaboration with the external evaluator to feed information on grant implementation and outcomes back to program stakeholders.

Implementing Change on Multiple Fronts Simultaneously

Because the key elements of the CBE approach encompass virtually all aspects of educational delivery, they force an institution to implement change on at least four fronts simultaneously. First, because credentials must reflect robust and valid competencies that are aligned to current industry requirements, the CBE approach forces change in curriculum development and maintenance. Curriculum developers must include industry more explicitly than in traditional education models because competencies must align with job skills requirements; moreover, they must undertake continuous maintenance of course content to ensure industry relevance. Sinclair used the Ohio IT standards—developed cooperatively by faculty disciplinary experts, state officials, and IT industry leaders—as its point of departure for developing program and course competencies. Beyond this, project leaders developed a "stakeholder collaborative" process to structure regular engagement with regional employers and other industry and workforce stakeholders, at both the executive and line manager levels. The collaborative process was designed to support alignment of the college's IT curriculum with both current and future labor market needs, which in turn should enhance regional economic development by ensuring that these needs are understood and met by the college.

Second, the primacy of assessment in CBE requires that tests be reliable and secure and measure job-relevant competencies, which can force change in assessment, as well as curriculum development. Sinclair faculty and instructional designers devoted a great deal of attention to mapping learning activities and assessments—in some cases, at the item level—to course and program competencies. They also required students be physically present at a Sinclair testing center to ensure assessment security. (The WGU model relies on online proctoring services, which Sinclair considered but did not implement.)

Third, the flexible pacing of the Sinclair CBE model required changes to institutional procedures. For example, enrollment and financial aid are traditionally structured around the academic calendar. Sinclair implemented an automated system for enrollment in which course sections were combined as students register for them throughout a term. Such a process allowed students to enroll after the traditional window closed and ensured that faculty had sufficient enrollments to support their target course load. Challenges arose for financial aid when a student registered and enrolled in flex-paced CBE courses sequentially within a term, rather than all at once at the beginning of the term. In such cases, a student could ultimately complete a "full-time" course load but not qualify for "full-time" financial aid, because the student was not enrolled full time at the point when aid was calculated. Similar issues arose for students using veteran's benefits. Program staff had to mediate between individual students and the relevant aid or benefits officers to ensure that students could access the aid for which they were eligible.

Finally, the independent and flexibly paced nature of the CBE student experience required a rethinking of student services and pedagogy. Students must work much more independently than in traditional models and must obtain and demonstrate a high level of competency on all key learning objectives. Sinclair used grant funds to hire academic coaches to provide enhanced and personalized supports to Accelerate IT students. Faculty teaching in the program must be certified to teach online and were guided by a handbook developed explicitly for teaching CBE courses.

The Sinclair Model: Sustainable by Design

In tackling the challenges posed by change on multiple fronts, Sinclair sought to operationalize CBE in a way that should lay the foundation for sustainable and measurable comprehensive change. Early in the grant, Sinclair and its partner colleges agreed to take on the following tasks across multiple areas of the institution (Person, Goble, & Bruch, 2014, p. 4):

1. "Develop a new and replicable CBE curriculum development process that will ensure that competencies, content, and assessments are continuously improved and widely disseminated.
2. Develop and provide new student support services that address the particular needs of . . . students in CBE programs.
3. Enhance the technological infrastructure for delivering CBE courses and assessments.
4. Offer a full suite of courses in several IT programs that lead to a series of stackable and latticed credentials with labor market value.
5. Address the organizational procedures and policies to allow students to progress through CBE programs of study that are delinked from traditional academic terms."

In developing their CBE model, Sinclair intentionally leveraged administrators, faculty, and staff in key institutional roles to ensure that college stakeholders would "own" the change and that the program could be sustained beyond the grant period. This approach was facilitated by the grant's project director who was the dean of distance learning and had also spearheaded the work under the prior NSF grants. Project leadership brought individuals in other key positions throughout the institution onto the grant, including course developers and instructional designers, as well as student support and career services staff. Indeed, the program relied on several key staff members who planned to remain at the college after the grant period.

Project leaders also leveraged existing institutional tools and processes, both to serve as a foundation for the CBE model and to support its integration, replication, and scale throughout the institution. They integrated CBE curriculum development into Sinclair's web course development department in the distance learning division. This integration facilitated course development with standardized tools and processes used for developing all online courses. At the same time, the explicit competency mapping processes that supported relevance and quality in CBE course content could be encouraged in all online courses. A cornerstone of the department and the CBE model is the master course model by which all Sinclair online courses were developed. This model employed a single course shell and a systematic and replicable course development process. Because it produced courses with the same organization and structure, the master course shell supported students' independent movement through fully online and flex-paced courses and instructors serving as mentors, both of which are key features of the CBE model.

Student support services were also integrated into the existing distance learning division. This integration allowed the services to benefit from the division's tools and processes. For example, the grant leveraged the division's "How to Succeed in an Online Course" as part of orientation for CBE students. At the same time, the grant funded a significant expansion of supports that can be integrated back into and potentially beyond the distance learning division. The grant allowed Sinclair to develop and implement a five-phase student support model that addressed admission, enrollment, retention, transition, and completion using a data-driven, tiered-support approach with automated routine interventions and targeted personal interventions. It also allowed Sinclair to package existing online career services tools into a "Virtual Career Center" that can be sustained after the grant through the college's central academic advising unit. Finally, it supported partnerships with other internal college completion initiatives to pilot learning management system attendance, dropboxes, and gradebook features in traditional (face-to-face) gatekeeper courses to enable targeted interventions there.

Employer and public workforce engagement, the final element of the Sinclair CBE model, was critical for ongoing job-relevance of competencies and support of student success in education and career. Project leaders used the grant to build upon existing organizational processes and structures. They engaged employers through existing program advisory boards and leveraged the existing business and public services internship program to provide credential-seeking students with the opportunity to apply classroom skills and competencies in the workplace. Beyond these efforts, they used the grant to adopt a "stakeholder collaborative" model that focused on regional economic development through collaboration between the college and key employer and industry partners to address current and future labor market needs. They enhanced engagement with the public workforce system by colocating the grant's career coach in the local American Job Center. Finally, they sought to align disparate engagement efforts by incorporating work under the TAACCCT grant into engagement efforts under the college's Title III "Connect 4 Completion" grant, which supported career communities and more holistic advising and where employers and public workforce partners participated in advisory teams.

Although program leaders successfully leveraged some college procedures under the grant, other procedures posed obstacles for the CBE model, although technology helped overcome some of these barriers. For example, course scheduling and staffing were challenged by the flex-paced approach of CBE, but project leaders integrated both into existing academic department processes and the college's registration and scheduling processes by using an automated filter to populate each instructional shell with students from the various registration sections. Similarly, project leaders automated intake, screening, and admission processes—which were more rigorous for Accelerate IT than for most other online programs—by integrating CBE orientation and approval processes into the existing approval processes for "How to Succeed in an Online Course." Not all procedural barriers could be addressed through technological solutions, however; some required manual solutions. For example, the challenge of securing financial aid and other benefits in flex-paced CBE courses still required staff to work with financial aid or other benefits officers.

Successes, Challenges, and Lessons Learned for Practice

Sinclair's experience with the Accelerate IT program offers many insights for other college leaders seeking to replicate its successes and mitigate against the challenges they are apt to face when structuring reform. The lessons may be especially relevant when CBE is to serve as a vehicle for comprehensive change.

The successes of the Accelerate IT program often stemmed from an intentional symbiosis: the grant-funded program benefitted from college resources and the college benefitted from grant resources. At the program's outset, existing state IT standards, Sinclair's master course model, and movement at the college toward competency-like course objectives supported a smooth transition to CBE. By drawing project leadership and key staff from existing positions at the college, the program could access a broader pool of resources than if it had staffed the program exclusively with grant funds. At the same time, these staff could share learning and adopt procedures developed under the grant more broadly within their home departments and divisions. This symbiosis helped to support, scale, and sustain the CBE model at Sinclair.

A culture of innovation at the college also seemed to influence Sinclair's success. Executive leadership actively fostered this culture, which was evidenced in the many innovative programs nurtured by the college (e.g., Completion by Design and Connect 4 Completion). In describing the college culture, program stakeholders depicted it as "experimental," noting that "it's okay to fail." Within the context of the Accelerate IT program, this culture of innovation allowed stakeholders to iterate on the flex-paced, competency-based model, learning from near-term failures to build long-term success. For example, when Accelerate IT was first launched, staff used a commercial assessment to determine students' readiness for online courses. When they found the commercial product was not a good predictor of their students' success, they replaced it with a home-grown computer literacy assessment and course.

Some of the program's challenges appeared to stem from the same sources as its key successes: existing college processes and institutional culture. Cultural challenges often stemmed from common conceptions of the faculty role in curriculum development. For example, a dean who was deeply involved in the development of the Accelerate IT software testing program described it as violating the many "thou shalt nots" of the college culture because program leaders pushed to develop the new program in 5 months instead of the more typical 1-year timeline and structured it as a single course to meet all industry certification requirements instead of the multiple-course model desired by faculty. Although this particular example ended successfully, overcoming the institutional culture required executive sponsorship far beyond what academic programs might normally expect. Similarly, attitudes toward faculty autonomy resulted in some initial misunderstanding around the involvement of academic coaches in monitoring student progress. After a period of adjustment, however, faculty and coaches worked in partnership to monitor student progress.

Both the college's internal organizational environment and external requirements posed challenges to comprehensive change. For example, project leaders did not have complete flexibility in staffing CBE courses, given institutional rules around course loads and salaries and federal rules around benefits.

Extrapolating from Sinclair's successes and challenges provides several lessons for community colleges. First, CBE programs will likely require changes to community college institutional procedures and culture. Because such procedures and culture are sometimes abstract, implicit, or even unseen, Sinclair's example encourages us to consider three concrete factors:

1. Timing. The timing for change needs to be right. In particular, stake-holders must have arrived at what one program leader called a "pain point," where failure to implement change would carry its own neg-ative ramifications. In Sinclair's case, the transition by the state legis-lature to completion funding served as such a catalyst for change.
2. Leadership and Influence. Executive leadership is necessary but not sufficient for program success. It can allow those who seek change to break or bend institutional rules (i.e., to violate the "thou shalt nots"), and help obtain buy-in from key stakeholders. In addition, front-line program staff also need to have what one Sinclair stakeholder termed a "strategic presence" on the various committees and working groups whose buy-in is important.
3. Work Planning. Precisely because culture and procedures can be ab-stract, implicit, or unseen, changing them requires not only a mul-tipronged approach, as Sinclair demonstrates, but also a clear sense of the path toward results. As Accelerate IT program leaders put it, "You can't go from the Wild West to CBE in one step" and "Trying to skip steps is always problematic." As such, community college lead-ers need to work within their institutional structure and culture with clear work plans, ideally driven by a strong theory of change and con-crete program logic model.

A second lesson from Sinclair is that CBE models both required and supported a culture of inquiry, because job-relevant competencies are al-ways evolving. Ensuring the relevance of competencies required careful monitoring of students' education and career outcomes. At the same time, student learning was constantly assessed in CBE models, so actionable data are readily available. Still, as Maxwell and Person describe (Chapter 9 of this volume), having data and using data for improvement are not the same thing. College leaders contemplating adoption of CBE models should be prepared to invest time, attention, and material resources in data-driven continuous improvement processes, supported by a strong understanding of the relationships between inputs, activities, and results.

A third and final lesson is that CBE models—at least those that share key characteristics of Accelerate IT—are not necessarily appropriate for all students or for all faculty. In particular, when CBE is flexibly paced, it re-quires a great deal of maturity, organization, and motivation on the student's part. To address this reality, Sinclair implemented careful intake processes that tried to prepare students for the challenge and to redirect those who were unwilling or unable to meet it. For faculty, CBE requires a willingness to move away from publisher content as a major organizing principle for their courses and an openness to a different kind of relationship to students and employers. The latter is true regardless of whether the model is flex paced. As Brock and colleagues note (Chapter 2 of this volume), faculty are central to the success of virtually any comprehensive change and may be

NEW DIRECTIONS FOR COMMUNITY COLLEGES • DOI: 10.1002/cc

key to sustaining it. It is therefore important to gain the buy-in and participation of a critical mass among them. Because CBE is not appropriate for or attractive to all students and faculty, it may need to be offered alongside more traditionally structured programs. Even so, its focus on precisely articulated and relevant competencies can be widely adopted, even in "traditional" classroom settings to help support student learning and education and career success.

References

Johnstone, S. M., & Soares, L. (2014). Principles for developing competency-based education programs. *Change: The Magazine of Higher Learning, 46*(2), 12–19.

Person, A. E., Goble, L., & Bruch, J. (2014). *Developing competency-based program models in three community colleges.* Oakland, CA: Mathematica Policy Research.

Person, A. E., Goble, L., Bruch, J., & Mazeika, J. (2015). *Implementing competency-based education in community colleges: Findings from the evaluation of a TAACCCT grant.* Oakland, CA: Mathematica Policy Research.

Ann E. Person *is a senior researcher at Mathematica Policy Research.*

Nancy Thibeault *is the former dean of distance learning and instructional support at Sinclair Community College in Dayton, Ohio.*

9

This chapter discusses challenges to using data in a continuous improvement framework and describes the approaches some community colleges have used to overcome those challenges.

Using Data for Continuous Program Improvement

Nan L. Maxwell, Ann E. Person

Current comprehensive reform efforts unfold within complex institutional contexts, are influenced by local and macroeconomic factors, and respond to stakeholder needs. Because these forces are constantly changing, successful educational programs must continuously adapt to new circumstances. As local economies shift their direction, as macroeconomic factors change the nature of work, and as stakeholders modify their views of what defines success, the success of reform efforts depends on an ongoing assessment of whether programs are achieving the goals set for student success and, if they are not, how they can identify and exploit opportunities for improvement so that goals can be met.

Such an environment suggests that comprehensive reform will be most successful if colleges use data to continuously assess programs and processes against observed student success indicators and undertake changes to improve programs and processes when success is not achieved. Reform leaders must recognize that, without building a culture that emphasizes continuous improvement and providing a measurement and assessment system to support it, reform efforts are unlikely to succeed. As scholars of the Achieving the Dream (ATD) effort concluded, "even large-scale reforms will not produce change if new innovations are ineffective" (Mayer, Cerna, Cullinan, Fong, & Rutschow, 2014). It is not enough to set high goals for student success and institute reforms designed to achieve them, colleges must also determine if and how programs are achieving the goals, identify the factors that challenge and facilitate their ability to meet them, and implement necessary corrections to ensure they are met.

This chapter offers a continuous improvement framework for colleges to use when engaging in comprehensive reform and describes the key challenges they face in adopting and building a measurement and assessment

NEW DIRECTIONS FOR COMMUNITY COLLEGES, no. 176, Winter 2016 © 2016 Wiley Periodicals, Inc.
Published online in Wiley Online Library (wileyonlinelibrary.com) • DOI: 10.1002/cc.20226

system to support such efforts. It draws challenges and lessons learned from a series of technical assistance activities designed to build measurement and assessment capacity among the U.S. Department of Labor (DOL) Round 1 Trade Adjustment Assistance Community College and Career Training (TAACCCT) grantees. Although the TAACCCT program emphasized particular aspects of reform (Bragg & Krismer, Chapter 6 of this volume), the lessons from it may apply across reform efforts more generally.

Continuous Improvement Framework

A continuous improvement framework is characterized by incremental improvements to ongoing processes (Deming, 1994; Temponi, 2005). It systematically evaluates key systems, processes, and outcomes by creating a basis for the strategic and continual improvement of performance. Although many different frameworks for continuous improvement exist, most share a focus on three main components: (a) goal setting, (b) measurement and assessment, and (c) information feedback (Chaplot, Booth, & Johnstone, 2013; Loeb & Plank, 2008).

Goal Setting.   Colleges must set specific goals for success that evolve from its institutional context, address both student and other stakeholder needs, and can be measured using quantifiable indicators of success. A college might, for example, set a goal that 75% of students attain a credential within 1 year after entering a program of study and obtain employment in the field of study within 2 months after receiving the credential. Both goals require the college to identify the sequenced coursework, supports, and services to help students attain credentials and become employed in their field. Both goals can be measured and have clearly identified links between them and the means to achieve them so areas for improvement can be identified if goals are not met.

Measurement and Assessment System.   Measurement and assessment efforts typically occur at the program level to understand and document student success and identify facilitators and challenges to success. For example, because course sequencing and availability are essential to completing a credential within 1 year, the measurement and assessment system should determine whether students can easily enroll in the courses they need when they need them as well as whether credentials are completed within 1 year. Identifying practices and processes alongside outcomes is essential to understanding facilitators and challenges to success. Measurement of both student success and program processes must begin at the start of reform so as to provide a baseline against which reform outcomes can be compared to help track process changes following reform.

Examining indicators of student success and program processes requires that colleges have an appropriate infrastructure and the capacity to collect and assess valid data. Without high-quality data—including quantitative measures of student success and quantitative or qualitative measures of program processes—the continuous improvement process is undermined because decision making might be based on inaccurate or incomplete information. Furthermore, information might be misconstrued or misused unless it is analyzed appropriately and presented in a manner that supports application to program decisions.

Information Feedback. Colleges must ensure that results from the measurement and assessment system are fed back into strategic and improvement processes and that decision makers have the flexibility and incentives to use the information. Even the strongest measurement and assessment system will be ineffective if the information from it is not used to ensure program goals are met and appropriate. If indicators of success suggest that programs met their goals and the processes were implemented as expected, stakeholders would refine processes that might produce better outcomes or develop plans to replicate the program in a different area or to scale it to reach more students. Alternatively, if indicators of success show that programs did not meet their established goals or that processes were not implemented as planned, colleges would implement changes to improve success.

Goals and indicators of success might evolve and change over time, as new information is gained through the measurement and assessment process, and in reaction to shifting environments. An effective continuous improvement process will examine indicators against current goals but also against changing environments to identify ways to strengthen programs and processes to ensure ongoing student success. Such strengthening does not occur in a one-shot assessment, but through a systematic process of inquiry, assessment, and enhancement (Chaplot et al., 2013).

Application of the Framework in Community Colleges

We used this continuous improvement framework to determine if the 32 community colleges with Round 1 TAACCCT grants had a measurement and assessment infrastructure to support the reforms they were implementing. This research stemmed from a technical assistance effort, funded by the Bill & Melinda Gates Foundation, to support measurement and assessment (Maxwell, Person, & Bruch, 2013). Although DOL did not require Round 1 TAACCCT-funded colleges to have a third-party evaluator that might help them establish or improve such processes, they were required to track performance measures for program improvement, including seven DOL-defined outcomes for participants and a comparison cohort of students not in TAACCCT-funded programs.

From May to October 2012, about 6 months to 1 year after grants were awarded, the study team collected information from five sources to assess each college's needs for measurement and assessment assistance and to provide insights into their ability to engage in a continuous improvement process. Information sources included (a) a review of all 32 grant proposals; (b) an online survey of measurement and assessment assistance needs, completed by 19 grantees; (c) semistructured telephone interviews with 43 stakeholders across 29 grantees to assess the implementation status of TAACCCT-funded programs, measurement and assessment plans, and grantee concerns and needs; (d) a measurement and assessment planning worksheet reviewed in person with 20 grantees; and (e) visits to eight colleges to provide measurement and assessment technical assistance.

Challenges to Colleges' Engagement in Continuous Improvement

Our research suggested that, 9 months after the grants were awarded, none of the 32 colleges had a complete continuous improvement framework to assess and enhance the programs for which they received funding. Four critical challenges emerged with some, but not all, aligning with the three main components of a continuous improvement framework.

First, much like colleges in Completion by Design (Brock, Mayer, & Rutschow, Chapter 2 of this volume) and Virginia's developmental education reform (Edgecombe, Chapter 3 of this volume), many colleges lacked a unified vision for change, which threatened their ability to set and achieve goals. About 60% said they did not need assistance in developing a theory of change or its visual representation in a logic model, which can be used to create a shared vision that helps define program goals and guides reform. Yet their descriptions of programs were often too broad to set clear and measurable program goals—a dilemma that could be addressed by developing a logic model. For example, one grantee identified 99 combinations of TAACCCT program components and another identified 57, suggesting that the vision for change had not identified the most critical components. Had the grantees used a logic model to place these program components into a theory of change, they would have realized the need for a more explicit unifying framework to tie them together.

Second, colleges faced difficulty developing and applying key measures. About 9 months after the grant was awarded, nearly 85% of the colleges lacked a cohesive plan even for collecting—much less analyzing and interpreting—data on DOL-mandated student outcomes measures. Almost 80% reported needing assistance in securing the agreements necessary to obtain required data on employment outcomes and almost one third reported needing general data collection assistance. Further challenges arose in assessing program-specific goals because grant-mandated student outcomes were sometimes not aligned with the colleges' own learning goals and because many measures developed could not be quantified (38% proposed progress and 46% proposed implementation measures instead of outcome measures). Finally—and critically—11 months after the grant was awarded, only half the colleges could articulate a clear definition for a program participant, making it difficult to know for whom success should be measured.

Third, colleges struggled to structure measurement and assessment plans that would produce information to determine whether student success was achieved. Indeed, most plans included a pooled set of DOL-mandated student outcomes that would make it difficult to identify program-specific outcomes or mechanisms that could lead to effective changes. Furthermore, most could not articulate what they wanted the measurement and assessment system to capture. About 94% of applications failed to articulate research questions to assess whether relevant outcomes and implementation processes achieved stated goals, with the two grantees that identified research questions addressing only program implementation and not student outcomes. This omission occurred despite the explicit DOL requirement for grant applicants to "set performance targets and … collect data on participant characteristics, progress measures, and performance outcomes to continuously monitor and improve program performance" (U.S. Department of Labor, 2012, p. 27). By 6 months after the award, about 20% of grantees could articulate such questions though they did not necessarily have the data to address them.

Fourth, colleges faced challenges in fully implementing their programs in a timely manner. About 11 months after grants were awarded, only 11% had fully completed curricular materials, and just 6% had the necessary technology platforms or tools in place. Grantees showed more progress in staffing and recruiting students into programs, although only about one third had fully implemented these program components. Without the fundamental program components in place, it is difficult to engage in even a well-conceived continuous improvement process.

Successful Examples from the Field

Despite the challenges faced in bringing together the components needed for a measurement and assessment system, some colleges built and enhanced parts of the system. We discuss such successes using examples from three different consortia.

One consortium launched new programs in the aerospace industry with redesigned developmental education, enhanced support services, and curricula aligned to employer needs. Consortium leadership decided to prioritize DOL performance reporting on implementation, progress, and outcome measures. Because the consortium included 11 colleges with programs of varying length and credentials in five occupational fields, meeting the DOL requirements was a challenge. In particular, DOL's requirement that participant and comparison cohorts be balanced on gender posed problems, given the colleges' explicit goal of increasing female enrollments. Although the leadership was keen to learn about how implementation and outcomes varied across programs and colleges, they chose a pragmatic approach and focused their learning goals on the DOL-required measures and limited their sample for reporting to participants at the "lead college" in each of the five occupational fields. The consortium made measurement and assessment manageable by narrowing the focus in the first year of the grant and anchoring their approach in the local college context.

A different consortium, composed of 10 community colleges, offered accelerated developmental education, ongoing academic and career guidance, and stackable credentials in four advanced manufacturing career fields. Leadership engaged stakeholders early in the grant and contracted with a faculty member to assess the program. The evaluator, a sociology professor at a local university, worked with the project during the grant's first year and helped them identify assessment priorities to validate their theory of action and provide continuous feedback for program improvement. During the first year of the grant, the project manager refined the assessment priorities to focus on employment, including job placement, and worked with the evaluator to identify a strong comparison group by which to measure success. Engaging someone with assessment expertise early in the process allowed program staff to have considerable control over the assessment design, which helped ensure findings were accessible and useful to stakeholders.

A third example came from a statewide consortium funded to develop short certificate modules and degree programs with online and hybrid courses in four health services career pathways. During the initial stages of implementation, it became clear that the original grant writers and the grant implementers did not share the same vision for the program. Although the relationship among grant priorities, programs, strategies, and outcomes was clear to the executive director and members of the grant-writing team, they were not clear to college staff. Consortium leadership engaged a team of researchers to initiate a logic modeling process that allowed college staff at each campus to map the links between grant strategies, program components, and outcomes as they developed and implemented the program. Colleges continued to flesh out the logic model in the grant's second year as they linked specific actions to each strategy and identified the outcomes most relevant to their programs. The process helped staff focus their goals and objectives, and ultimately helped the consortium learn how program components might affect student outcomes.

Lessons Learned

Our examination of the Round 1 TAACCCT grantees' capacity to use data for continuous improvement uncovered three lessons for community colleges seeking to assess comprehensive reform efforts: create a shared vision for comprehensive reform, dedicate adequate resources for measurement and assessment, and ensure measurement and assessment systems provide information aligned with reform goals. We elaborate on each in turn.

Create a Shared Vision for Comprehensive Reform. The DOL Round 1 TAACCCT solicitation for grant applications (SGA) encouraged applicants to rethink how they do business with a long list of "priorities" and "strategies." In response, some grantees designed programs that lacked a coherent vision to tie their program components together and, as a result, could not always articulate what their grant-funded program was or how it was supposed to work. Furthermore, the links between program components, students in the program, and expected outcomes were not explicit.

Colleges needed to engage in a process to develop and communicate a shared vision. The logic modeling process (described in the section Challenges to Colleges' Engagement in Continuous Improvement) is one way to help ensure a common vision that encompasses all program components and articulates how they should work together toward a set of well-defined and achievable goals. It can also support program implementation and help focus measurement and assessment resources, leaving college stakeholders better positioned to engage in a continuous improvement process.

Dedicate Adequate Resources to Measurement and Assessment. One common challenge arose from a failure to appreciate the level of effort and particular skills needed to assess complex programs that are changing with reform. A substantial number of colleges did not budget for any measurement or assessment activities beyond those required for DOL performance reporting and others budgeted for them at a much lower level than allowed. Yet internal data collection and analytic capacity were not always adequate. Although some colleges had staff with strong analytic capacity, many lacked staff with appropriate analytic skills to think about systematic collection of qualitative information and boosting the rigor of quantitative approaches.

An effective continuous improvement process also requires the means to apply the right analytic approach at the right time and, although most colleges could apply descriptive analytics, they did not have the capacity to structure analytics to the stage of program development. For most colleges, implementation was in the early stages and outcomes had not yet materialized, or program goals were not well defined, which meant programs were not yet at a stage in which measurement of implementation or outcomes would produce useful information. Colleges need to recognize that when comparisons of outcomes to program goals are undertaken too soon they might underestimate their ultimate impact and lead colleges to mistakenly interpret the findings as program failure instead of program formation.

An obvious solution to this set of challenges is for colleges to identify and fund adequate analytic expertise. Unfortunately, in tight fiscal environments, such a solution is not always feasible. Creative solutions to such shortages include using resources from external sources (e.g., faculty at the college or local universities, ATD, the Community College Research Center, and the Office of Community College Research and Leadership), although in the long run, it is important that colleges build an internal capacity and not rely solely on the services of external experts.

Ensure Systems Provide Information that Aligns with Program Goals. Community colleges must develop measurement and assessment systems alongside the reform process to ensure reforms achieve the goals for student success and to identify program components that produce those successes or that need modifying to enhance success. Building functioning measurement and assessment systems cannot occur overnight and must unfold in stages, much like restructuring programs under comprehensive reform. In the early stages of program development, measurement and assessment systems might best document challenges in a manner that can support further program development and maturation. As programs mature, a mature—and institutionalized—measurement and assessment system can evaluate implementation and outcomes against program goals within a fully functioning continuous improvement framework that engages multiple stakeholders.

The short-term cost of diverting scarce resources away from programs and toward a measurement and assessment system might seem daunting as reform efforts get underway. The cost of not doing so may be high in the long term, however, if programs developed and implemented during reforms cannot identify which innovations effectively improve student outcomes, which do not, and which need modifying with changes in the environment. Comprehensive reform can only improve student success if it can identify the drivers of success and challenges to it, and can use this information to continuously improve programs by tracking indicators of student success, comparing the indicators against program goals, and assessing the need to modify program implementation and/or goals.

References

Chaplot, P., Booth, K., & Johnstone, R. (2013). Building a culture of inquiry: Using a cycle of exploring research and data to improve student success. Retrieved from http://inquiry2improvement.com/attachments/article/12/CbD-Building.pdf

Deming, W. E. (1994). The need for change. *Journal for Quality and Participation, 17*(7), 30–32.

Loeb, S., & Plank, D. N. (2008). *Learning what works: Continuous improvement in California's education system.* Stanford, CA: Policy Analysis for California Education, University of California. Retrieved from http://www.edpolicyinca.org/publications/learning-what-works-continuous-improvement-california%E2%80%99s-education-system

Maxwell, N., Person, A. E., & Bruch, J. (2013). *Evaluation and measurement for TAAC-CCT grant programs: Recommendations and resources for getting started.* Oakland, CA: Mathematica Policy Research. Retrieved from http://www.mathematica-mpr.com/our-publications-and-findings/publications/evaluation-and-measurement-for-taaccct-grant-programs-recommendations-and-resources-for-getting-started

Mayer, A. K., Cerna, O., Cullinan, D., Fong, K., & Rutschow, E. (2014). Moving ahead with institutional change: Lessons from the first round of Achieving the Dream community colleges. New York: MDRC. Retrieved from: http://www.mdrc.org/sites/default/files/moving_ahead_with_institutional_change_fr_0.pdf

Temponi, C. (2005). Continuous improvement framework: Implications for academia. *Quality Assurance in Education*, *13*(1), 17–36. Retrieved from http://dx.doi.org/10.1108/09684880510578632

U.S. Department of Labor, Employment and Training Administration. (2012). *Notice of availability of funds and solicitation for grant applications for Trade Adjustment Assistance Community College and Career Training Grants Program*, SGA/DFA PY-12-10. Retrieved from http://www.doleta.gov/grants/pdf/taaccct_sga_dfa_py_12_10.pdf

NAN L. MAXWELL *and* ANN E. PERSON *are senior researchers at Mathematica Policy Research.*

10

This chapter describes the challenges and practical barriers community colleges face when implementing comprehensive reform, exploring how reforms are leading to some improvements but not often scaled improvements.

Implementing Comprehensive Reform: Implications for Practice

Karen A. Stout

Can comprehensive community colleges reform comprehensively? In theory, the reforms noted in this volume, if implemented as a package, should produce significant institutional improvements in student course completion, progression, and attainment of a credential that has labor market value and/or leads to successful transfer and baccalaureate completion. Yet, to date, we lack systemic and significant improvements in outcomes across these metrics. Although some interventions show signs of promise, and we have many hypotheses for what a system of interventions might look like, we lack a proven framework for comprehensive redesign. The lack of a comprehensive framework is not for lack of effort. Community colleges across the country are intentionally redesigning in many areas. However, the reform is often at the margins or in pockets without the changes in culture and organizational design that produce scaled results.

Comprehensive reform is achievable if leaders at all levels—national state, and local—are able and willing to take the necessary steps. These steps include creating a compelling and unified case for change, calling for and expecting better results, and mobilizing key internal and external stakeholders as champions for the difficult work of comprehensive reform. Most important, leaders must work to "craft coherence" to mobilize and connect reform from within the field to the calls for reform coming from outside the field. These combined forces should be aligned and synchronized. Too often those on the ground are not engaged in reform or do not see a compelling case for reform. Thus, they see changes as discrete, forced, and unconnected to their own work.

This chapter explores how reforms lead to some improvements, but not scaled improvements, and why comprehensive reform remains a challenge

NEW DIRECTIONS FOR COMMUNITY COLLEGES, no. 176, Winter 2016 © 2016 Wiley Periodicals, Inc.
Published online in Wiley Online Library (wileyonlinelibrary.com) • DOI: 10.1002/cc.20227

and a leadership imperative. It applies a blended framework for driving reform from Achieving the Dream (ATD) and the American Association of Community Colleges (AACC) to the work at Montgomery County Community College (Pennsylvania) to illustrate reform in action.

The Context

Colleges operate in environments that vary from community to community and from state to state. Colleges also operate within a national dialogue that has focused heavily on accountability and, most recently, completion. Understanding this context is important to understanding the challenges colleges face in implementing comprehensive reform.

National.   Several national frameworks for reform exist, including ATD and Completion by Design (described in Brock, Mayer, & Rutschow, Chapter 2 of this volume). However, their compatibilities are uncertain and they often collide with one another, causing fragmentation and confusion in reform at the state and local levels. The lack of a common metaframework for reform means that local practitioners must craft their own theory of change, borrowing from those in the field, and customizing the framework to their local context.

State.   Many states, eager for accelerated results, have jumped into the reform movement. Some have legislated the elimination of developmental education (e.g., Florida). Others take a comprehensive approach to reform with legislation touching on dual enrollment, remediation, completion, and transfer (e.g., California, as described by Friedmann, Kurlaender, & VanOmmeren, Chapter 4, and Thor & Moreau, Chapter 7 of this volume). Still others offer incentives to colleges to reform with performance-based funding models (Tennessee offers one example). The contextual variance in these models makes it difficult to apply lessons learned across states and to say with certainty which piece or pieces of each state reform model drive results.

Institutional.   At the institutional level, discrete interventions focused on a singular reform, such as developmental education, do not have the results required for enough students to achieve equitable progression and completion. Colleges have discovered, through trial and error, that more comprehensive and connected approaches are required, including approaches that focus on student pathways and approaches that address college readiness comprehensively (as described by Bragg & Krismer, Chapter 6, and Friedmann et al., Chapter 4 of this volume).

Framing Reform

Montgomery County Community College provides a concrete example in conceptualizing and understanding comprehensive reform in community colleges. Montgomery is a suburban, multicampus college located just outside Philadelphia in a Pennsylvania county with nearly 900,000 residents. The service area is diverse economically and ethnically. In 2014, the college served about 25,000 credit students at two primary locations, a culinary arts institute and a public safety training center, and a virtual campus. Transfer has always been central to the college's mission, but the program portfolio also includes occupational certificates, certifications, and degrees.

In 2006, the college joined ATD. Eight years later, it received ATD's Leah Meyer Austin award for its adoption of "whole college" solutions to improve student success. The college's student success journey was not linear, not cohesive, and not without struggles. It was filled with modest and incremental successes. It is the story of many of our nation's strong and striving community colleges on the cusp of significant improvement in student success outcomes.

Joining ATD offered Montgomery a framework to organize and advance change, as well as leadership coaching and technical assistance to begin and sustain the work. This framework, later blended with the AACC's recommendations from the 21st Century Commission report, further guided the college's reform approach.

The original ATD theory of change (Achieving the Dream, 2009) emerged from lessons learned from colleges joining ATD in the early stages of the reform movement and was anchored by five principles: (a) committed leadership; (b) use of evidence in identifying areas for improvement and measuring the success of resulting interventions; (c) broad engagement of key internal and external stakeholders; (d) systemic improvement that ties policy and practice together; and (e) a focus on equitable outcomes including disaggregating student outcomes data by race, ethnicity, and income.

The AACC theory of change is set forth in its April 2012 report titled *Reclaiming the American Dream: Community Colleges and the Nation's Future* (AACC, 2012). It includes seven principles within three broad areas of reform: (a) redesign—increasing completion and readiness and closing the skills gap, including eradication of attainment gaps associated with income, race, ethnicity, and gender; (b) reinvention—refocusing the mission and collaborating with partners in philanthropy, government, and the private sector; and (c) resetting—implementing policies and procedures that promote rigor and accountability for results.

Reform in Action

Montgomery's early ATD work focused on redesigning developmental education rather than systemic improvement of the full student experience. This strategy offered a protected way to wade into an otherwise threatening change process: it was on the margin and nonthreatening to faculty teaching college-level courses. In addition, it was in the area data indicated was most clearly in need of redesign. The college adopted strategies to accelerate progression through math and English developmental sequences, moved to multiple measures for course placement, fully redesigned and scaled the way the first-level math developmental course was taught (including comprehensive professional development for adjunct faculty), and worked with high school math faculty to align high school and college course outcomes.

As results of the developmental education work were celebrated, and as faculty in the middle of innovating received accolades and resources, the ripple effect of innovation engaged more faculty in piloting reform in areas with more potential for scale and reach. The Gateway Course Academy was founded to give faculty a methodology for digging into course data and refining pedagogy. Program faculty, using new analytical tools populated with newly available student outcomes data, started to unbundle pathways within the majors identifying and eliminating barriers to progression. Pilot student success efforts blossomed across the college, organized within the framework of the ATD work plan and AACC's principles for redesign. The college also learned that it did not have to meticulously replicate national research results before taking on already tested initiatives. The college inventoried 34 interventions in seven categories of reform: acceleration, accurate placement, course redesign, culture of evidence, engagement, policy, and student support systems. As it inventoried, it archived what worked and what did not work, as demonstrated by improvement on relevant success indicators outlined in the pilot design, and documented how the initiative was moved to scale or not. The reforms were anchored in the blended framework.

Committed Leadership (ATD)/Refocusing the Mission (AACC). The college president linked early student success work to the college's strategic plans and articulated and reinforced the metrics for success. She worked to connect initiatives, make a compelling case for the "why," and keep the attention of the college on student success. This vision and culture setting cannot be delegated. As one colleague advised, this is work that presidents must "keep in their pocket."

In addition, the board of trustees became connected to the work through their curriculum committee and newly introduced monthly student success reports to the full board. The President's Advisory Council on Diversity reviewed disaggregated student success data and led conversations around equity. Program advisory committees placed student outcomes data on programs at the center of their work. The president tied these conversations together and served as a constant advocate for building the student success movement on campus and in the community.

Use of Evidence (ATD)/Accountability for Results (AACC). A key to the college's success was building an analytic infrastructure to set a compelling rationale for the need for change, as well as a structure to measure and drive results. Its analytical infrastructure included five carefully connected building blocks: (a) a mission that explicitly values data-informed decision making; (b) a strategic and annual planning system with connected goals and objectives that cascade into performance management plans and faculty evaluation systems; (c) solid information technology, institutional effectiveness, and data governance systems and structures; (d) reporting tools that support wide dissemination of data; and (e) professional development around using analytics in decision making. This analytic approach supported the data-informed decision making required for comprehensive change, an approach already emphasized in this volume as foundational for advancing comprehensive reform.

Broad Engagement (ATD)/New Collaborations (AACC). Networks for faculty engagement were central to the design of the work at Montgomery. The Student Success Initiative Team (SSI) was formed in 2006 and remains the nexus and anchor for the reform work. The SSI is composed primarily of faculty with rotating membership depending on the emphasis and reach of the annual work plan. Several working groups are connected to the SSI and extend opportunities for involvement. This SSI network is fluid and nimble yet also connects to the academic governance structure and the formal organizational structure fostering innovation. Engagement extends outside the college through connections with school district superintendents, transfer partners, and the workforce community. New collaborations with donors and private funders have also resulted from a highly focused private fundraising campaign that raised $10.5 million for student success programs and scholarships.

Systemic Improvement (ATD)/Redesign to Increase Readiness and Completion (AACC). Redesign efforts drive policy and program review work. For example, a revised academic readiness policy allowed for placement based on multiple measures. Academic program reviews, built in response to the core student success data, have clarified, compressed, and simplified program pathways, by attending to corequisites and prerequisites and condensing credits for completion to 60 in all transfer programs.

Equity (ATD)/Eradication of Attainment Gaps (AACC). The minority male mentoring effort, originally targeting African American men, was accompanied by a fall-to-spring persistence increase to 78% for those in the program from 62% for those not in the program. In addition, changes to placement processes decreased the number of African American students enrolled in developmental education from 17% of the entering 2008 cohort to 9% of the entering 2012 cohort with no significant change in subsequent course success.

Comprehensive Reform 2.0

The college is now using the ATD/AACC framework to arrange its reforms along a continuum in five areas: (a) precollege interventions, (b) assessment/placement reforms, (c) curricular redesign, (d) academic supports, and (e) transitions. This approach ties reforms together in a cohesive package allowing for breadth, depth, and greater scale in strategy and implementation. Examples of work within each area follow.

Precollege Interventions.   The college works closely with K–12 partners to implement a focused dual enrollment strategy that built on school district desires and relied on carefully constructed pathway academies around health sciences, information technology, advanced manufacturing, and liberal arts and sciences transfer.

Assessment/Placement Reforms.   Using research from the Community College Research Center as a catalyst (Hodara, Jaggars, & Karp, 2012; Scott-Clayton, 2012), the college moved incrementally toward using multiple measures for student placement to improve accuracy. As a result, more students are placed directly into college-level math and English. As an example, in English, a combination of changes including implementing WritePlacer, lowering ACCUPLACER cutoff scores, and adding an SAT exemption reduced students requiring developmental English from nearly 40% of the fall 2008 cohort to less than 8% of the fall 2012 cohort.

Curriculum Redesign.   The redesign of the first-level developmental math class, Concepts of Numbers, led to significant (20% and better) advances in course success rates. That redesign is now being scaled nationally to 10 community colleges in five states and has served as a model at Montgomery for course redesign in other areas.

Academic Supports.   The college introduced an array of new academic supports (e.g., mentoring, supplemental instruction, and peer tutoring) and improved other supports (e.g., mandatory orientation, mandatory tutoring, and academic support labs). As of 2016, it is not yet clear which array of services works best for which students.

Transitions.   Transfer pathways were modified and simplified with a focus on building partnerships with selective admissions colleges to support the transfer of high-performing and low-income students. Student progress after leaving the college is now tracked using National Student Clearinghouse data, and transfer agreements are revised to support stronger baccalaureate completion if data indicate that students are not successful upon transfer.

The new effort that pulls the work in this continuum together, with reach and capacity for scale from the start, is the comprehensive redesign of student entry processes that will require every new credential-seeking student (as of fall 2015) to set forth an educational, financial, and career plan within the first few weeks of their first semester. Newly developed dashboard tools from the college's participation in the Integrated Planning and Advising System work (Jaggars & Karp, Chapter 5 of this volume) will allow students to monitor their progress against their goals and allow advisors and faculty to do the same.

Lessons from the Challenges to Change

Although critics are vocal about the slow pace of quantitative improvement in student progression and completion, qualitative improvement, such as significant changes in patterns of college behavior, often presents the first signs of progress. Since the reforms discussed here were instituted, Montgomery improved its use of data to inform decision making, moved successful pilots to scale, ensured broad engagement from faculty and advisors on the front end of a change effort, and implemented policies and practices to place more students into college-level courses. These signs are important because they are often cultural and they show when a college is positioned for accelerated quantitative improvement. These qualitative signs relate directly back to the ATD theory of change model. After nearly a decade of work, all five of ATD's core quantitative elements for transformation (leadership, culture of evidence, broad engagement, equity, and policies and practices for systemic improvement) are firmly in place. Still, getting to comprehensive quantitative results, primarily significant changes in credential and degree completion, remains a challenge for many reasons, detailed next.

Local Context Matters. Community colleges are designed to reflect the aspirations of the communities they serve. With many audiences, expectations, and competing and ambiguous metrics for success (some unrelated to student completion), it is difficult for leaders to establish and maintain the relentless focus necessary to drive and sustain change around student success. Success for a community college and for a community college leader is often determined by local context and local priorities unrelated to student success: boards often set success criteria that are more related to local context than to student success.

Leaders Must Navigate Organizational Design. Colleges operate as the organized anarchies described by Cohen and March (1974). In most colleges, the concept of command and control does not exist. Thus, a strategy for reform must wrap around the anarchy while also living at the center of it. The president must drive the reform with multiple constituents often controlling the pace and nature of reform. Navigating this tension toward productive results is a leadership art and requires balancing leading with a sense of urgency with a sense of patience. The need for this delicate balance is well articulated *Crisis and Opportunity: Aligning the Community College Presidency with Student Success* (Aspen Institute, 2013).

Governance and Unionization Can Complicate Reform. Shared governance and unionization (Montgomery balanced both) add another layer of complexity to the organizational design challenges. Many reforms touch on locus of control issues where faculty voice and management rights can collide. In addition, part-time faculty are often the first to innovate yet they may have little authority, recognition, reward, or support to drive change. Presidents and other college leaders must establish collaborative conditions and relational trust to lead reform at a pace that advances change yet does not bring the college into disequilibrium.

Reform May Require New Resources. A significant challenge is one of resources. Declines in public funding have come full force in the midst of the focus on student completion. At Montgomery, both local and state funding was cut significantly just after the college joined the ATD network. Funding student success interventions through reallocation is difficult, and perhaps impossible, and creates political tensions on campus. Current financial systems lack a strategic financing approach that can fully account for savings from reallocation, project the need for additional dollars, and budget for additional costs that cannot be absorbed by reallocation. The president must manage these internal tensions and manage new demands for increased engagement in private and alternative fundraising. Without support and without a strategic financing model, the demand to preserve institutional financial viability is difficult to balance with a focus on leading student success efforts.

Leadership Pipelines Pose Challenges.   Colleges are underresourced in talent, especially in key areas like institutional research and process improvement science, both competencies fundamental to comprehensive reform. In addition, stress from retirements and transitions in the pipeline of presidential and academic leadership are creating a crisis of continuity on many campuses making a sustained focus on student success nearly impossible.

Conclusion

Can comprehensive community colleges reform comprehensively? The answer remains elusive and depends on leadership at all levels. Leaders, funders, reformers, and policy makers must stay the course and build as many supports as possible to help community college presidents and the faculty and staff do the hard work on the ground to be successful. Every college story around reform will be different with varying sets of interventions. Some work will fail; some will succeed. We must tolerate this ambiguity. Most likely, the work will be grounded in a theory of change, borrowed from the national metaframeworks, and grounded in data, to fit local context. Colleges need more help in shaping their own institutional theory of change as well as action planning around student completion. Colleges will also need deeper technical assistance to build stronger capacity in core areas that align with their established theory of change (e.g., building a culture of evidence, engaging faculty, supporting equity, leveraging technology, redesigning student entry, using multiple measures for assessment, and aligning professional development with goals). This support may come from (a) learnings from the AACC led and newly launched work around pathways that builds on the ATD, Completion by Design, and AACC models of change; (b) adoption of ATD's updated theory of change, which adds a new focus on the teaching and learning environment and faculty leadership of change as well as customized support for colleges in specific capacity areas such as data/technology, equity, planning, and policy; (c) new but aligned investments from the philanthropic community and public funders in approaches that we know work (such as City University of New York's Accelerated Study in Associate Programs program) but for which resources are too thin to scale them; and (d) new federal (such as the recent approval to allow some dual enrollment students to receive federal financial aid) and state policy and resource support that advances practice in areas we know are successful. This level of support is still uncertain, but it will be essential for colleges to counteract the immense challenges of change articulated in this chapter and volume.

References

Achieving the Dream. (2009). *Field guide for improving student success.* Retrieved from http://achievingthedream.org/resource/178/field-guide-for-improving-student-success

American Association of Community Colleges [AACC]. (2012). *Reclaiming the American dream.* Retrieved from http://www.aacc.nche.edu/aboutcc/21stcenturyreport_old/index.html

Aspen Institute. (2013). *Crisis and opportunity: Aligning the community college presidency with student success.* Retrieved from https://www.aspeninstitute.org/publications/crisis-opportunity-aligning-community-college-presidency-student-success/

Cohen, M. D., & March, J. G. (1974). *Leadership and ambiguity: The American college president.* Hightstown. NJ: McGraw Hill.

Hodara, M., Jaggars, S. S., & Karp, M. M. (2012). *Improving developmental education assessment and placement lessons for community colleges across the country.* New York: Community College Research Center, Teachers College, Columbia University.

Scott-Clayton, J. (2012). *Do high stakes placement exams predict college success?* New York: Community College Research Center, Teachers College, Columbia University.

KAREN A. STOUT *was the president of Montgomery County Community College (PA) from 2001 to 2015 and is currently the president and chief executive officer of Achieving the Dream, Inc.*

NEW DIRECTIONS FOR COMMUNITY COLLEGES • DOI: 10.1002/cc

INDEX

Accelerated Learning Program (ALP), 15

Accelerated Study in Associate Program (ASAP), 18, 35

Achieving the Dream (ATD), 7, 14, 23–27, 89, 100; and community college reform, 15; early implementation of, 25–27; Lumina Foundation for Education and, 14

Ackoff, R., 74

Alliance for Quality Career Pathways (AQCP), 65

American Association of Community Colleges (AACC), 100

Baccalaureate, 64

Bailey, T., 9, 11, 12, 13, 14, 21, 35

Bailey, T. R., 13, 14, 17, 53, 54, 56, 60

Baker, E. D., 35

Baker, R., 54

Balu, R., 31

Barnett, E. A., 55, 56

Barragan, M., 35, 41, 55, 60

Bauer-Maglin, N., 18

Belfield, C., 11, 16

Belfield, C. R., 42

Bettinger, E. P., 54

Bickerstaff, S., 41, 55, 60

Bill & Melinda Gates Foundation, 7, 12, 15, 23, 27, 80

Bird, K., 64

Booth, K., 90, 91

Bork, R. H., 55, 60

Bragg, D., 9, 17

Bragg, D. D., 63, 64, 65, 72, 80, 90, 100

Brock, T., 7, 9, 14, 15, 16, 23–26, 33, 36, 39, 54, 55, 70, 80, 86, 92, 100

Broek, M., 47

Bruch, J., 79, 82, 91

Bryk, A. S., 41

Butte-Glenn community college, 75

Byndloss, C. D., 15, 16

California Community College (CCC), 45, 51, 73; assessment rates and coursetaking, 48–49; craft method, 74–76; EAP program's adoption and implementation, 45–51; findings, 50; moving online technologies, 76–78; planning for reform, 45–46; reform efforts, 46–48

California Master Plan for Higher Education of 1960, 12

California's Common Core State Standards, 47

California State University (CSU), 45, 76

Campus Computing Project, 76

Cantu, L., 64

Career pathways, 63–65; career-focused curriculum and instruction, 64; in community colleges, 65–66; competency-based core curriculum, 64; contextualized developmental education, 65; credit attainment, 65; intensive support services, 65; stackable credentials, 64

Carnevale, A. P., 13

Center for Law and Social Policy (CLASP), 65

Cerna, O., 7, 15, 16, 24, 25, 26, 89

Chamberlain, A., 31

Chaplot, P., 90, 91

Cheung, A., 31

Cho, S. W., 14, 15, 28, 35, 42, 55

Cincinnati State Technical and Community College, 66

City Colleges of Chicago (CCC), 18

City University of New York (CUNY), 17

Cohen, M. D., 105

College 101, 55

College completion, 12–13; developmental education, 14; intake and supports, 13–14; programs, 13

Community college, 13–14

Community college, comprehensive reform in, 31–32, 99–100, 106–107; ATD, 23–27; CBD, 27–29; challenges to change, 104–106; comprehensive reform 2.0, 103–104; framing reform, 100–101; reform in action, 101–103; role of research, 30–31

Community College Research Center (CCRC), 25, 57

Volcanoes

Anne Schreiber

NATIONAL
GEOGRAPHIC

Washington, D.C.

—A.S.

Published by National Geographic Partners, LLC, Washington, D.C. 20036.
All rights reserved. Reproduction in whole or in part without written permission
of the publisher is prohibited.

Library of Congress Cataloging-in-Publication Data

Schreiber, Anne.
Volcanoes! / by Anne Schreiber.
p. cm. -- (National geographic readers series)
ISBN 978-1-4263-0285-5 (trade paper : alk. paper) -- ISBN 978-1-4263-0287-9
(library : alk. paper)
1. Volcanoes -- Juvenile literature. I. Title.
QE521.3.S34 2008
551.21--dc22
2007049743

Front Cover, 24 (top), 32 (top, right): © Digital Vision; 1: © Robert Glusic/Digital Vision/Getty Images; 2: © Shutterstock; 4-5: © Bruce Davidson/npl/Minden Pictures; 6, 32 (center, left): © Stuart Armstrong; 7, 32 (bottom, right): © Bryan Lowry/SeaPics.com; 8-9: © Yann Arthus-Bertrand/CORBIS; 9 (inset), 12-13: © Martin S. Walz; 10: © Doug Perrine/SeaPics.com; 11: © Pierre Vauthey/CORBIS SYGMA; 14 (top): © WEDA/epa/CORBIS; 14 (bottom): © Goodshoot/CORBIS; 15 (top): Mike Doukas and Julie Griswold/USGS; 15 (bottom), 32 (bottom, right): © Pete Oxford/Minden Pictures/Getty Images; 16 (inset), 27 (top): JPL/NASA; 16-17: © Phil Degginger/Mira.com/drr.net; 18-19: K. Segerstrom/USGS; 20-21: © Francesco Ruggeri/Getty Images; 22 (inset), 32 (top, left): Cyrus Read/AVO/USGS; 22-23: Gateway to Astronaut Photography of the Earth/JSC/NASA; 24 (bottom): © J.D. Griggs/CORBIS; 25 (top): © CORBIS; 25 (bottom): © Rebecca Freeman/Tulane University; 26: © John Stanmeyer/VII; 27 (center): © H. Poitrenaud/AFP/Getty Images; 27 (bottom): © Art Wolfe/The Image Bank/Getty Images; 28: © John Cornforth/SeaPics.com; 29 (top): © John Harvey Photos: 29 (center): © Joseph Van Os/The Image Bank/Getty Images; 29 (bottom): © Bo Zaunders/CORBIS; 30-31: © Norbert Rosing/National Geographic Image Collection, 32 (center, right): © Jeremy Horner/CORBIS.

National Geographic supports K–12 educators with ELA Common Core Resources.
Visit natgeoed.org/commoncore for more information.

Table of Contents

Mountains of Fire!

Ash and steam pour out of the mountain. Hot melted rock rises up inside the mountain. Suddenly a spray of glowing hot ash shoots out. It is an eruption!

More melted rock is forced out. It spills down the side of the volcano in a burning hot river. Anything that cannot move is burned or buried.

KIMANURA VOLCANO
ZAIRE

WORD BLAST

ERUPTION: When magma reaches Earth's surface. Some eruptions are explosive.

5

Hot Rocks

When magma comes
out of the Earth it is
called lava.
The lava hardens.
Ash and rock pile up.
A volcano is born.

ASH

VENT

LAVA

MAGMA
CHAMBER

Deep beneath the Earth's surface it is hot. Hot enough to melt rock. When rock melts it becomes a thick liquid called magma. Sometimes it puddles together in a magma chamber. Sometimes it finds cracks to travel through. If magma travels through a crack to the surface, the place it comes out is called a vent.

 **WORD BLAST**

MAGMA: Thick, liquid melted rock.
MAGMA CHAMBER: A space deep underground filled with melted rock.
VENT: Any opening in Earth's surface where volcanic materials come out.

Shaky Plates

Where do cracks and vents
in the Earth come from?

The land we live on is broken into pieces
called plates. The plates fit Earth like a
puzzle. They are always moving a few
inches a year. When plates pull apart...
or smash together...watch out!

This picture shows the gap that forms when plates pull apart.

THINGVELLIR, ICELAND

NORTH AMERICA

EUROPE

Atlantic Ocean

AFRICA

SOUTH AMERICA

Pacific Ocean

— Earth's Plates

Mid-Atlantic Ridge

One place where Earth's plates smash together is called the Mid-Atlantic Ridge. It is the longest mountain range on Earth and most of it is underwater.

An Island Is Born

What happens when two plates pull apart?
They make a giant crack in the Earth.
Magma can rise up through these cracks.
This even happens underwater.

About 60 million years ago an underwater volcano poured out so much lava, it made new land. A huge island grew, right in the middle of the ocean. Lava formed the country of Iceland!

SURTSEY

About 50 years ago, people saw smoke coming out of the ocean near Iceland. A new island was being born right before their eyes! They called it Surtsey, after the Norse god of fire.

The Ring of Fire

Karymsky Volcano

ASIA

Pacific Ocea

Indian Ocean

Mount Merapi

Ring of Fire
Earth's plates
Mountains
Active volcanoes

AUSTRALIA

What happens when plates bump into each other? Maybe a mountain will be pushed a little higher. Maybe a volcano will erupt. There may be an earthquake, or a tsunami, or both!

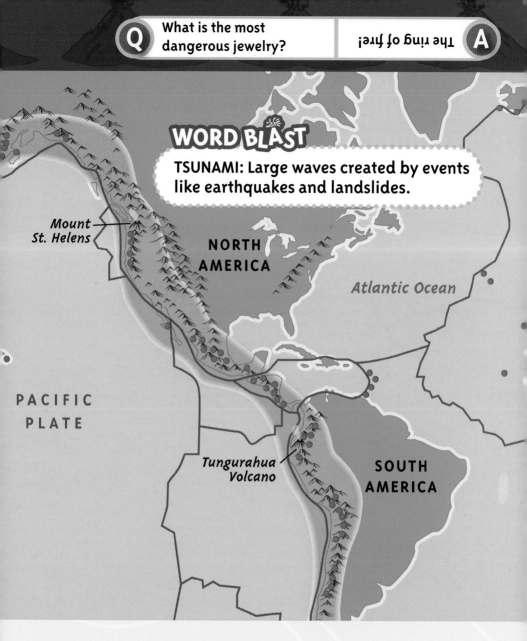

WORD BLAST

TSUNAMI: Large waves created by events like earthquakes and landslides.

Mount St. Helens

NORTH AMERICA

Atlantic Ocean

PACIFIC PLATE

Tungurahua Volcano

SOUTH AMERICA

The edge of the Pacific plate is grinding into the plates around it. The area is called the Ring of Fire. Many of Earth's earthquakes and volcanoes happen in the Ring of Fire.

Postcards from the Ring

I Lava YOU!

Mount Merapi, Indonesia

Moose You Very Much!

Karymsky Volcano, Kamchatka

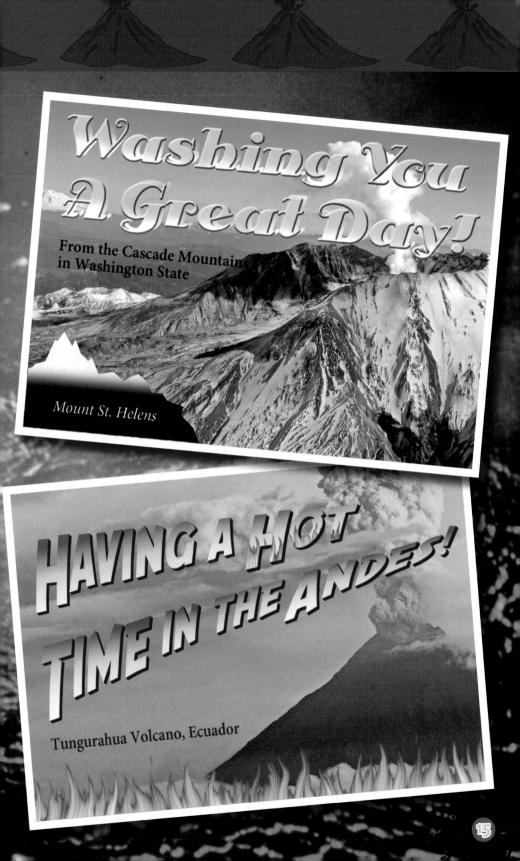

Washing You A Great Day!

From the Cascade Mountains in Washington State

Mount St. Helens

HAVING A HOT TIME IN THE ANDES!

Tungurahua Volcano, Ecuador

Meet a Volcano... or Three

Not all volcanoes are the same. What kind they are depends on how they erupt.

The lava from a shield volcano is hot and liquid. Rivers of lava flow from the volcano's vents. These lava flows create a gently sloping volcano.

HOT FACT

Olympus Mons on Mars is a shield volcano. It is the largest volcano in our solar system! Seen from above, it is round, like a shield.

MAUNA LOA

The Hawaiian myth of Pele tells the story of how Pele, goddess of earth and fire, built a home on Mauna Loa. Violent volcanic eruptions are said to be Pele losing her temper.

Meet Mauna Loa!

PARICUTIN VOLCANO

A cone volcano has straight sides and tall, steep slopes. These volcanoes have beautiful eruptions. Hot ash and rocks shoot high into the air. Lava flows from the cone.

One day a cone volcano started erupting in a field in Mexico. It erupted for nine years. When it stopped it was almost as high as the Empire State Building.

Meet Paricutin!

HOT FACT

Even though Paricutin stopped exploding in 1952, the ground around it is still hot! Scientists guess that Paricutin spit out 10 trillion pounds of ash and rock.

A stratovolcano is like a layer cake. First, lava shoots out and coats the mountain. Then come rock and ash. Then, more lava. The mountain builds up with layers of lava, rock, and ash.

Meet Mount Etna!

MOUNT ETNA, ITALY

There is a myth about Vulcan, a Roman god of fire and iron. He lived under Vulcan Island, near Mount Etna. Every time Vulcan pounded his hammer, a volcano erupted. The word *volcano* comes from the name Vulcan.

The True Story Of Crater Lake

Crater Lake may seem like a regular lake, but it is actually a stratovolcano. It was once a mountain called Mount Mazama. Now it is a deep, clear lake in Oregon.

An explosion over 6,000 years ago blew the top off Mount Mazama. Lava, dust, and ash swept down the mountain. The mountaintop fell in and a giant caldera was formed. Over time the caldera, a crater, filled with water. It is the deepest lake in the United States.

WORD BLAST

CALDERA: A caldera is formed when the top of a volcano caves in.

CRATER LAKE

After the mountain collapsed, there were more eruptions. In one, a small cinder cone of ash and lava was formed. This cinder cone pokes out of the lake. It is called Wizard Island.

Volcanoes Rock!

PAHOEHOE

NAME: Pahoehoe (say Pa-hoy-hoy)

HOW IT FORMS: Fast, hot, liquid lava hardens into smooth rope-like rock.

SPECIAL POWER: It hardens into beautiful and weird shapes known as Lava Sculptures.

AA

NAME: Aa (say Ah-ah)

HOW IT FORMS: The crust on top of Aa lava hardens into sharp mounds of rocks.

SPECIAL POWER: It can cut right through the bottom of your shoes!

24

PELE'S HAIR

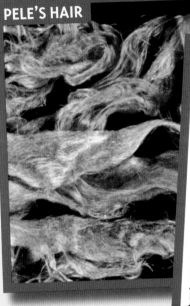

NAME: Pele's Hair (say Pel-lay)

HOW IT FORMS: Lava fountains throw lava into the air where small bits stretch out and form glass threads.

SPECIAL POWER: These strands of volcanic glass are super thin and long, just like hair! Small tear-shaped pieces of glass, called Pele's tears, sometimes form at the end of Pele's Hair.

PUMICE

NAME: Pumice (say Puh-miss)

HOW IT FORMS: In a big explosion, molten rock can get filled with gas from the volcano. When the lava hardens the gas is trapped inside.

SPECIAL POWER: The gas makes the rock so light, it can float on water.

Volcanic
Record Breakers

Indonesia, a string of islands in the Ring of Fire, has **more erupting volcanoes** than anywhere else on Earth.

JAVA ISLAND

The place with the **most volcanic activity** is not on Earth. It is on Io, one of Jupiter's moons!

The 1883 explosion of Krakatau was the **loudest sound** in recorded time. People heard the explosion over 2,500 miles away. Anak Krakatau, which means "Child of Krakatau," is a volcano that was born in 1927 where Krakatau used to be.

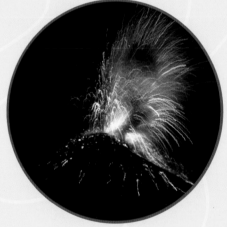

Mount Etna is the **largest active volcano** in Europe.

27

Hot Spots

Do you want to visit somewhere really hot? Check out these hot spots—places on Earth where magma finds its way through the Earth's crust. Hot spots are heated by volcanic activity!

The Hawaiian Islands are all volcanic mountains. They start on the sea floor and poke out above the sea. Kilauea in Hawai'i is still erupting. As long as it keeps erupting the island of Hawai'i keeps growing.

On Kyushu Island, in Japan, some people use the hot springs to boil their eggs.

Take a bath with the monkeys in Japan.

In Iceland, you can swim in pools heated by volcanoes.

Exploding Ending

If you visit Yellowstone National Park, you will be standing on one of the biggest supervolcanoes on Earth. Yellowstone sits on an ancient caldera. Magma still bubbles and boils a few miles below ground.

Yellowstone has a lot of geysers—more than 300. The magma below Yellowstone caldera heats underground water. The water boils and bursts to the surface as geysers, spraying steam and hot water high into the air.

Go to Yellowstone and see Earth in action!

CALDERA
A caldera is formed when the top of a volcano caves in.

MAGMA
Thick, liquid melted rock.

MAGMA CHAMBER
A space deep underground filled with melted rock.

TSUNAMI
Large waves created by events like earthquakes and landslides.

ERUPTION
When magma reaches Earth's surface. Some eruptions are explosive.

VENT
Any opening in Earth's surface where volcanic materials come out.

DEDICATION
To my cherished family, Kristin and Mike, Amanda
and Kevin, Maura and Todd; and to my favorite little people:
my grandsons, Stephen, Oliver, Eamon, and Rogers...and my
grandniece and grandnephew, Ada and Owen. Thank you for
filling my life with such joy. I love you all dearly.

In memory of my beloved husband, Steve,
who continues to inspire me every day.

In thanksgiving to God for His abundant
blessings and constant support.

ACKNOWLEDGMENTS
In grateful appreciation to Jean Christen and Etta Wilson, whose
wisdom, guidance, faith and friendship are such blessings to me.

With a heart full of thanks to my assistant and daughter,
Kristin Adams Litke, for all of her support and expertise.

To Harvest House Publishers
for believing in this story.

4

It was early morning at the Chatham Fish Pier. The sun was just starting to rise over the water, and the fishermen were getting ready for the day.

On board his boat, *Big Red*, Captain Steve checked his lobster traps. He planned to spend the day pulling his traps up from the ocean floor to see if he had caught any lobsters to sell back at the fish pier.

When everything was ready, Captain Steve started the engine and slowly moved out into the ocean.

A long way off shore and deep beneath the blue green waters was a large coral reef, where lots of fish, plants, and animals lived. And within the coral reef was the town of Shellville.

The morning sun was just peeking into the rocks where the Scallop family lived. Sammy stretched as he got out of bed, very excited. Sammy was in the fifth grade and was the catcher on his baseball team. Today was the championship game between Sammy's team, the Shellville Whitecaps, and the Spongetown Sluggers.

His little sister, Samantha, was in the first grade. She couldn't wait to cheer Sammy on in the big game.

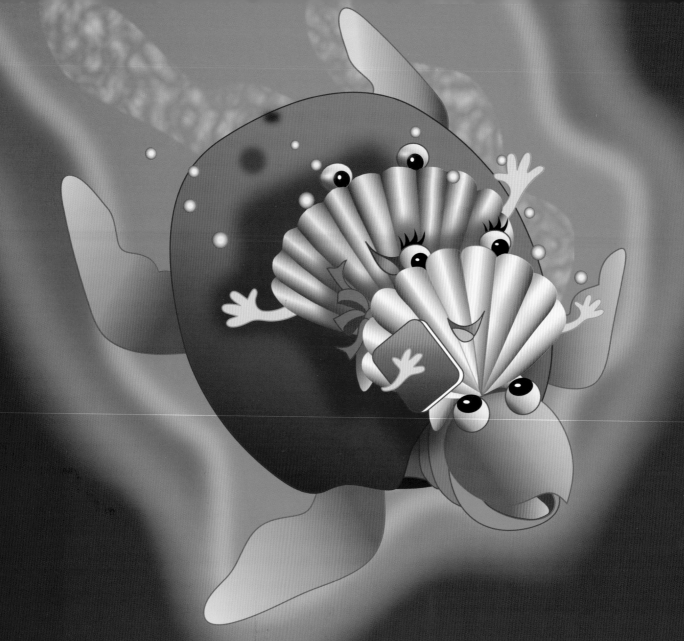

Soon they heard, "Anyone home?" It was their friend, Timothy Turtle, coming to see if they wanted a ride to school.

"Hey, Timmy," Sammy said. "We're just about ready." They kissed Mama and Papa Scallop goodbye and hopped onto Timothy's shell.

When they got to Reef Shellementary School, Sammy got in line with his friends Ollie Octopus, Suzie Snail, Casey Conch, Freddie Fiddler, Sally Starfish, Kelly Cod, and Timothy Turtle.

Sammy said good morning to his teacher, Miss Lucy Lobster. She made every day fun, as they studied dolphin songs, ocean rocks and the history of sunken treasure. They even learned how to ride seahorses.

The day went fast, and soon it was time for the big baseball game. In the bottom of the last inning, the score was tied as Sammy came to bat. On the first pitch, Sammy swung hard. "Strike One!" called Henry Hermit.

On the next pitch, Sammy swung with all his might and hit the ball so hard it went flying over the outfield and into the coral reef. It was a home run! His team won the championship! The crowd was cheering as Sammy ran around the bases and was hoisted up on his teammates' shoulders. Sammy was so happy.

A few days later, Sammy and Samantha were going home from school when Sammy heard a noise above him. He looked up just in time to see a big anchor coming down fast right above them.

Captain Steve had stopped to check his lobster traps and was dropping the anchor to hold his boat in place.

Sammy shouted, "Look out!" and quickly pushed Samantha out of the way. But before he could get away, the anchor hit the top of Sammy's shell and broke off a little piece.

"Ouch!" cried Sammy. As he rubbed the top of his head, he could feel the sharp edge where his shell had broken.

When they got home, Samantha told her parents how Sammy had saved her life. They hugged Sammy and told him they were so proud of him. Mama Scallop put an ice pack on his head to make it feel a little better.

The following day, Sammy's classmates saw his broken shell and laughed at him. No one remembered his home run or what a good friend he was. They all made fun of him, except for Timothy Turtle.

At lunchtime, only Timothy would sit next to Sammy. He felt so sad and alone. Tears fell from his eyes. Sammy wondered if he would ever have his friends back again.

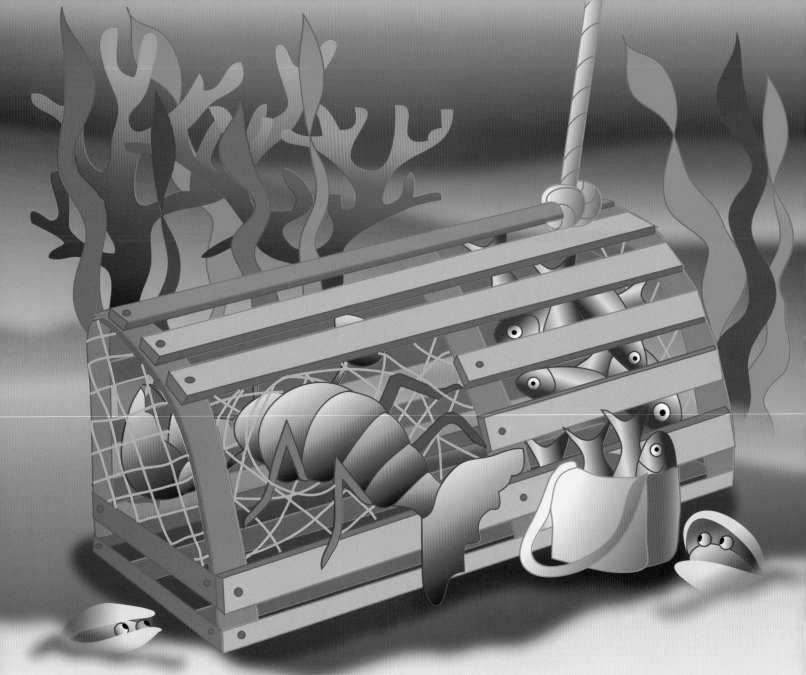

One afternoon Sammy's teacher, Miss Lucy, went grocery shopping in the coral reef. She smelled her favorite fish and followed the scent to a strange looking wooden box. Miss Lucy saw the herring inside the box behind some rope. She found an opening in the side of the box, so she crawled inside to reach the herring. But when she turned around to leave, she couldn't get out. She was stuck inside one of Captain Steve's lobster traps!

"Help! Help!" Miss Lucy yelled at the top of her voice.

Sadie Seahorse came by and tried to help. "I'm sorry, Miss Lucy, I don't have teeth sharp enough to cut the ropes and get you out." Others from Shellville came by too, but no one could figure out how to save Miss Lucy.

Sammy and Samantha had stopped at the park that day to play after school. When they heard a lot of noise coming from a large crowd nearby, Sammy pushed his way through and saw Miss Lucy stuck in the middle of the lobster trap.

"Don't cry, Miss Lucy," he said. "I'll try to cut you free."

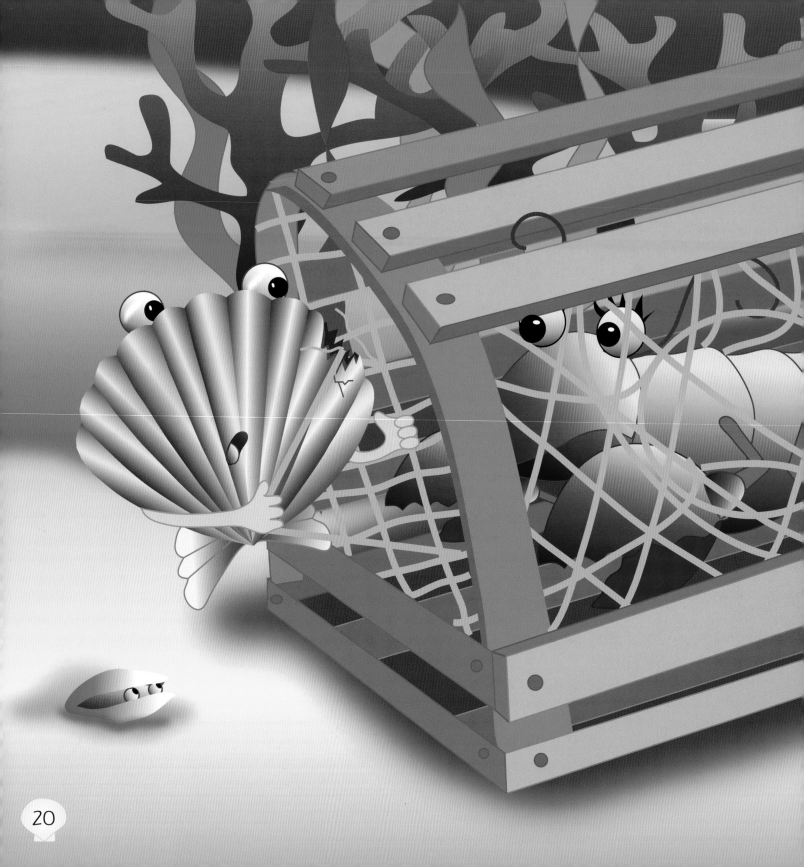

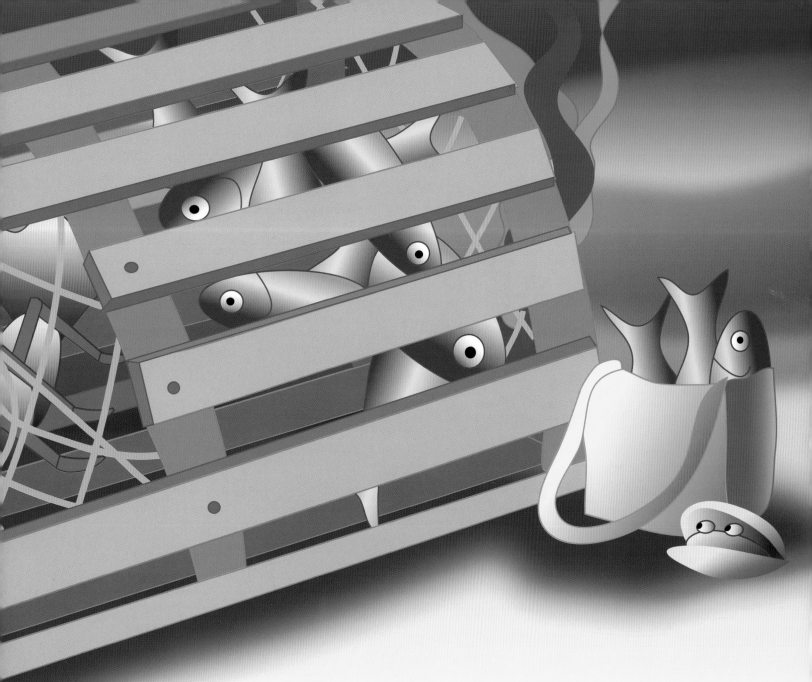

Sammy climbed onto the rope on the side of the lobster trap. He saw he would have to cut a big hole in the rope to free Miss Lucy. So Sammy held on tightly, put the sharp edge of his broken shell next to the rope, and started moving back and forth as hard as he could. Soon the rope started to break. First one piece... then another. Only a little more and Miss Lucy would be free.

Just then, the lobster trap jerked and turned onto its side.
"What's happening?" cried Miss Lucy.

Captain Steve was back checking his lobster traps again. He was
pulling Miss Lucy's trap up off the ocean floor.

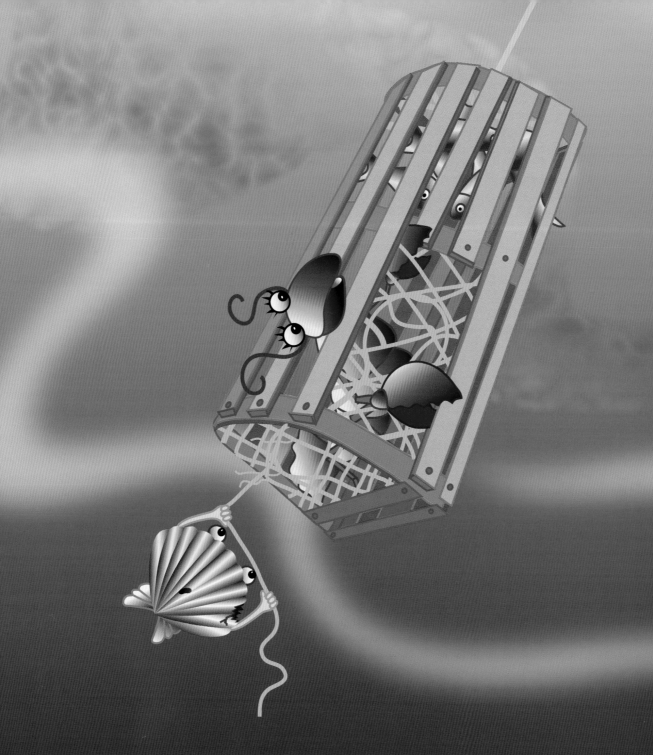

Sammy's eyes grew wide, but he held on with all his might.

The lobster trap rose higher and higher in the water.

23

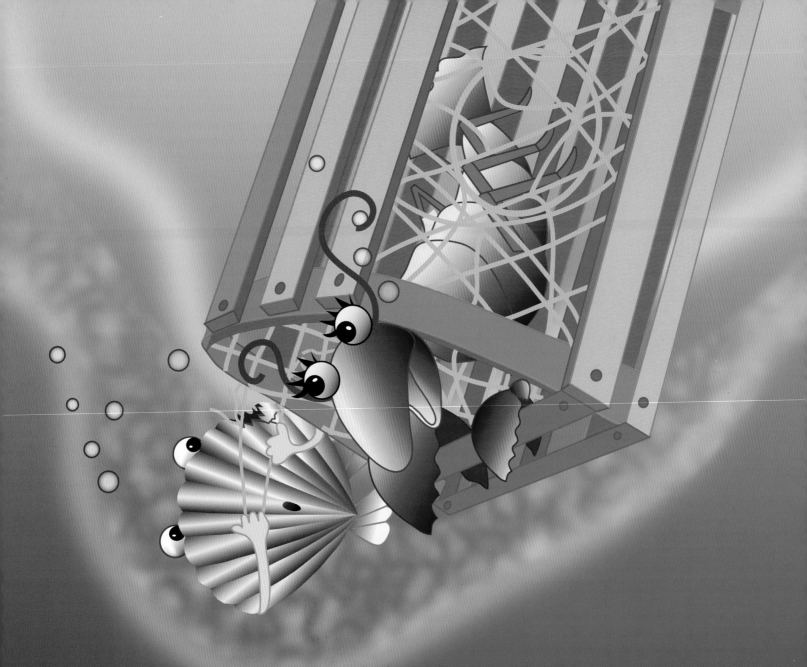

Sammy quickly put his broken shell onto the rope again and moved back and forth as fast as he could. If only he could save Miss Lucy!

Suddenly, Sammy heard "Snap!" Another piece of rope had broken. Finally the hole was big enough for Miss Lucy to squeeze through.

24

Sammy grabbed her claw and pulled her out, just before the lobster trap reached Captain Steve's boat. As they floated back down to Shellville, they could hear their friends cheering.

"Hip! Hip! HOORAY!"

everyone shouted, as Sammy looked around and smiled.

The next day at school, there was a big celebration in honor of Sammy. Miss Lucy called him to the front of the room.

The Sammy Award

"I know all of us are so proud of Sammy," Miss Lucy said. "He risked his life to save mine yesterday. But he also taught us a very important lesson...that it doesn't matter what we look like on the outside. What matters most is what we are like on the inside, in our hearts. Even if we are broken like Sammy or feel different or sad, we can still do great things. The very gifts that make us different may help others the most, just like Sammy's broken shell. What's important is to know that no matter what we look like or feel like, we are all very special people,

JUST THE WAY WE ARE.

"Reef Shellementary School is now going to give an award every month to the student who does something brave or kind for someone else. It will be called 'The Sammy Award.'"

Ollie Octopus stood up in the front row and started clapping. Soon everyone was cheering for Sammy. His classmates apologized for making fun of him.

"That's okay," Sammy said. "I'm glad to have you as my friends again."

Timothy Turtle was beaming as he brought Sammy some ice cream and the party began.

They had a lot to celebrate!

Questions for parents and teachers to encourage discussion with children on the main points of the story

1. Did Sammy have a lot of friends before he broke his shell?

2. How was Sammy treated in school after he broke his shell?

3. How did it make Sammy feel?

4. Was anyone a good friend to Sammy after he broke his shell?

5. Have you ever felt sad or alone like Sammy?

6. If so, what made you feel that way?

7. Did anyone make you feel better?

8. How did they do that?

9. Do you know someone who doesn't have many friends at school?

10. How can you help that person feel better?

11. How would that make you feel?

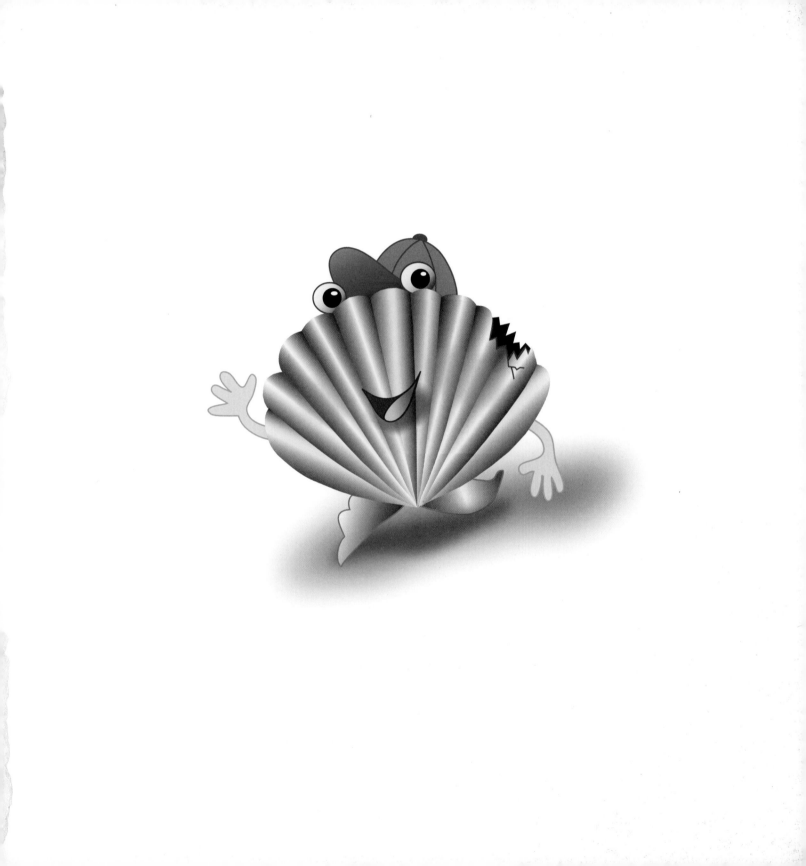